BUCKSKINS,
BULLETS,
AND
BUSINESS

Recent Titles in
Contributions to the Study of Popular Culture

BUCKSKINS, BULLETS, AND BUSINESS

A HISTORY OF BUFFALO BILL'S WILD WEST

Sarah J. Blackstone

CONTRIBUTIONS TO THE STUDY OF POPULAR CULTURE,
NUMBER 14

GREENWOOD PRESS
New York • Westport, Connecticut • London

Library of Congress Cataloging-in-Publication Data

Blackstone, Sarah J., 1954–
  Buckskins, bullets, and business.

  (Contributions to the study of popular culture,
ISSN 0198–9871 ; no. 14)
  Bibliography: p.
  Includes index.
  1. Buffalo Bill's Wild West Company—History.
2. Bill, Buffalo, 1846–1917. 3. Entertainers—
United States—Biography. I. Title. II. Series.
GV1821.B8B57 1986   978'02'0924 [B] 85-17760
ISBN 0–313–24596–7 (lib. bdg. : alk. paper)

Library of Congress Catalog Card Number: 85–17760
ISBN: 0–313–24596–7
ISSN: 0198–9871

First published in 1986

Greenwood Press, Inc.
88 Post Road West
Westport, Connecticut 06881

Printed in the United States of America

The paper used in this book complies with the
Permanent Paper Standard issued by the National
Information Standards Organization (Z39.48–1984).

10 9 8 7 6 5 4 3 2 1

For My Family

CONTENTS

LIST OF
ILLUSTRATIONS

Illustrations follow p. 76

Diagram of the Wild West grounds.

Setting up on the Wild West grounds.

Wild West grounds seen from the Eiffel Tower, 1889.

The artillery drill, Buffalo Bill's Wild West, 1907.

The buffalo hunt as part of "A Day at TE Ranch," Buffalo Bill's Wild West, 1907.

The life-saving drill, Buffalo Bill's Wild West, 1903.

Arabian acrobats, featuring the Whirling Dervish, 1907.

The Pony Express event, Buffalo Bill's Wild West, 1907.

Woman riding a bucking horse, 1907.

The bicycle jumping event, 1903.

The Battle of Summit Springs, Buffalo Bill's Wild West, 1907.

ACKNOWLEDGMENTS

No work of this type would ever be completed without the help of librarians, museum curators, and collections' supervisors. Therefore, I would like to thank the staff of the Western History Collection, the Denver Public Library; the Buffalo Bill Historical Center; the library of the Circus World Museum; the Special Collections Archive, University of Wyoming; the photograph collection of the Wyoming State Archives; the University of Oklahoma Archives; and Scout's Rest Ranch State Park. I would especially like to thank Paul Fees, curator of the Buffalo Bill Museum, Buffalo Bill Historical Center; Dick Flint, president of the Circus Historical Society; Barbara Rogers; and India Cooper.

In addition, I wish to express my appreciation to the Graduate Faculty of Northwestern University's Theatre Department for their support of my original idea to write this history of Buffalo Bill's Wild West and especially to Dr. Robert Schneideman and Dr. Linda Jenkins.

I owe a special debt of gratitude to the University of Central Arkansas for the faculty research grant which allowed me to complete my research and prepare the manuscript for publication.

BUCKSKINS,
BULLETS,
AND
BUSINESS

INTRODUCTION: FIRST IMPRESSIONS

Between the years 1882, when Colonel William F. Cody began organizing the first Wild West, and 1913, when he finally went bankrupt, the millions of people who saw his show in a dozen countries were exposed to a version of the winning of the West that claimed to be genuine but was in fact based almost entirely on illusion. This show was being performed by men and women who had actually participated in the Western movement and who claimed to be giving truthful and realistic performances of actual events, which gave the resulting mythic version of life on the frontier the weight and influence of truth. But the show was full-blown propaganda—glorifying the process of the winning of the American West and declaring to the world that America had won a resounding victory in its efforts to subdue the wilderness. The back-breaking, bloody, and often fatal task of taming the frontier was romanticized and glorified by Cody through his Wild West until the truth was so totally mixed with the myth as to be indistinguishable. The image that Americans have of themselves and the image that Europeans have of Americans is closely tied to both the reality and the myth of the American West.

By the time Cody opened his first Wild West show in May 1883, the land between the Missouri River and the Sierra Nevada was accessible to anyone who wished to settle there. Two transcontinental railroads were complete, and two more were under construction. The Homestead Act and the accompanying land acts had opened up all the Western lands except Oklahoma for settlement, and barbed wire had ended the open-range cattle industry, making small ranching and farming possible again.

The lawless mining camps, railroad boomtowns, and cow towns had either disappeared or become law-abiding communities within newly formed territories or states. The last of the hostile Indians had been defeated and moved to reservations. The frontier had begun to be a functioning part of the United States. By 1913, when Colonel Cody's celebrated show was put up for auction, this process was all but complete. All the Western territories had become states, and America would soon join its allies in fighting World War I.

During his lifetime William F. Cody participated in almost every phase of this settlement. As a boy he served as a messenger for the freight company of Majors and Russell, accompanied a wagon train of freight from Kansas to Colorado, and rode for the Pony Express. As he grew older, he served as a soldier in the Union Army, drove a stagecoach, and hunted buffalo to feed the crews laying the track of the Kansas Pacific Railroad. He was hired as a scout for the U.S. Cavalry in 1868. Cody participated in several major battles with the Indians of the northern plains (including War Bonnet Creek and Summit Springs) while serving in this capacity.

Later in his life, Cody took up a career as a melodrama actor, performing in his own troupe (the Buffalo Bill Combination) during the winter months and scouting for the army in the summer. Some of the profits from his acting career went to purchase Scout's Rest Ranch near North Platte, Nebraska, where he built a spacious home for his wife. In 1872 he was elected to a seat in the Nebraska State Legislature, an office he soon resigned. Beginning in 1883 Cody concentrated his energies on managing and starring in his Wild West, but he continued to encourage the settlement and development of the West. Between 1883 and his death in 1917, Buffalo Bill established the town of Cody, founded a stage line between Cody and Yellowstone Park, bought and maintained a working ranch near Cody, started an irrigation company in the Big Horn Basin, bought a gold mine in Arizona, started a film company that made Western films, and worked at a hundred smaller projects all intended to bring people to the West.

The years that Colonel Cody toured with his Wild West show brought many changes to the West he had known and had chosen to represent in his show. By the time the Wild West achieved its greatest success at the World's Fair of 1893, all but four of the Western territories had become states, the last Indian uprising had been quelled, and there were four transcontinental railroads. However, his show had great appeal for those in the Eastern United States and Europe who still imagined the West as it had been only twenty years before.

The audiences that saw Buffalo Bill's Wild West, in Europe and the Eastern United States, had already formed a view of the West that was both romantic and mythic but rarely accurate. The source of their "knowledge" of the west was threefold. First, they had the accounts of those who had gone west, through their letters, visits, travel accounts, guidebooks, and emigration newspapers. Second, they had pamphlets, brochures, and lectures of land speculators for the railroads and Western states. Finally, they had fictionalized accounts of novelists and playwrights. From these accounts arose the myth of the American West. The myth itself contained two different images. On one side was the image of the West as hostile and barbaric, and on the other was the image of the West as a place of promise and opportunity. William F. Cody presented a show that fit neatly into this myth, reinforcing both views of the West in each three-hour performance.

The most effective of the image makers who prepared the way for Cody were the people who had gone west to settle on the land being given away in America. Their letters home were vivid accounts of life on the Western frontier, and everyone in the community eventually heard these letters read out loud. There were hundreds of thousands of letters, all telling of wealth and success in the New World. The "America Letters" were perhaps the most accurate source of information available to the people of Europe, but even these were suspect. What emigrant could resist some exaggeration of his status in his new community to impress his friends and family and to encourage more people to join him in the West? Yet the effect of these letters was great, not only on the Europeans who decided to immigrate, but on those who stayed home and dreamed about a place where hard work was rewarded and everyone could succeed.

The image created by the America Letters was supported by returning emigrants who flocked to Europe to flaunt their success. They appeared in their villages dressed in American finery telling tales of their wonderful lives in the New World. These tales were suspect in the same way as the America Letters, but few, if any, Europeans doubted the evidence of their own eyes and ears. If Hans, or Anna, or Johann said it was so, then it was so.

Added to these very personal sources of information were the guidebooks published by Europeans who had visited the West or who knew someone who had visited the West. These books were published by the hundreds between 1825 and 1865 and were widely read.

The guidebooks published by those who had never been to the West were the least accurate but no less widely read. The books written by those who had traveled in America had built-in problems of their own. Many of the authors of these guidebooks traveled to America to prove or disprove the virtues of democracy and tended to print information that supported their views.

Closely allied to the guidebooks, but more readily available to the average European, were the emigration newspapers. These were sold cheaply and contained practical information on travel, land purchases, and farming. But once again the spectre of inaccuracy crept in. Most of their information came from successful emigrants seeking to increase the size of their communities and thus to increase land values. Again, the European eager for information was at the mercy of those eager to enhance land values, make money, or preach politics.

The already muddy impressions of Western America being received by Europeans were further confused by land speculators who came to Europe by the hundreds, ready to tell any tale of success to sell their property. Speculating companies eager to sell lands in Texas began this process in the 1840s. Soon private companies were joined by railroads and newly formed states to bring people and revenue to the New World.

The most successful of these land speculators were the land grant railroads. In order to build their lines the railroads needed capital. They raised this capital by encouraging emigration to farms on their land to be purchased before leaving Europe if possible and upon arrival if not. Each railroad maintained armies of agents in Europe; the Northern Pacific, for instance, had 955 agents scattered across Europe in 1883. These agents gave lectures, had posters printed and hung, distributed colorful brochures, and answered any and all questions put to them. A certain amount of accuracy was required because word of all-out fraud would reach Europe through other companies' agents, but the object was to sell land, and salesmanship was certainly practiced.

Individual states got into the business of selling land at almost the same time as the railroads because settlers meant money in the form of tax payments and exportable agricultural goods. No more honest than the railroads in their claims for their lands on the frontier, the states often worked side by side with other land speculation companies to lure Europeans to America.

Almost all these sources of information about America painted a picture of plenty and ease, a place where only hard work was necessary to attain success. Stories of hardship and danger overcome were left to the novelist. These novels were eagerly read by relatives of Western settlers who were anxious to understand what their loved ones might be experiencing, even though the books were only fiction.

The first novels about American frontier life to reach Europe were the *Leatherstocking Tales* of James Fenimore Cooper. Cooper attained immediate success in Europe, and his novels were seen as accurate reflections of the lives of frontiersmen and Indians. His novels also served as emotional safety valves that allowed people caught in the first waves of industrialization to escape the factories and the cities into an imagined outdoor world where physical activity, strength, and chivalry were prized above all other qualities.

American novels spawned European imitations, and soon a panoply of novels about the West was available in all the languages of the Old World. These books were strictly adventure tales with no moral messages about the plight of the Indian or the despoiling of the land.

By the early 1870s the Western was a part of the regular reading fare of most Europeans, and the stage was set for the entrance of the American dime novel which inundated Europe in the 1870s and 1880s. These novels were turned out by the thousands in America and soon were being copied by European authors in every country.

Dime novels followed a clear-cut formula of good against evil in stock Western settings. Anyone with a vivid imagination and a good sense of how to maintain suspense and excitement could write successful novels of this kind. For instance, Karl May, a German novelist who had never been to America, wrote 35 block-buster Westerns that earned him the title of "Germany's James Fenimore Cooper." His books were translated into twenty languages and read by 300 million people. They made him the favorite author of Adolf Hitler and Albert Einstein. Karl May might have been the most popular writer of Westerns in Germany, but his success was matched by other novelists across Europe. And there were many writers of lesser popularity flooding the market with their visions of the West.

Creating heroes and villains for these novels was not difficult. The heroes had to be glamorous, civilized enough to show human triumph over nature, and primitive enough to show human ability to live without bosses, factories, and cities. The villains had to be so savage as to show no hint of civilization and so mean and nasty that they unquestionably deserved the fate meted out by the hero at the end of the book.

Authors were further helped in their creations by the existence of certain types by which to model their heroes and villains. On the villain's side were half-breeds, Mexicans, white renegades, buffalo hunters, Mormon elders, "pirates of the prairies," and Yankees. On the hero's side were hunters, soldiers, ranchers, eastern "greenhorns," bee hunters, and wood runners. Many of these types were based on people in real life; others came strictly from the author's imagination.

Of all the hero types, two were favored above all the rest: the hunter (based on Cooper's Natty Bumpo) and the plainsman (created as the frontier left the woods and moved out over the prairie). Both wore buckskin shirts and were skilled in the use of knife and rifle, and both were noble enough to represent civilization's triumph over the wilderness but savage enough to enjoy maiming the villains.

In the Eastern United States people not only had the eye-

witness accounts of the emigrants, the propaganda of land speculators, and the tales of the novelists, they also had the melodrama
to help them form their impressions of the West. These melodramas followed much the same pattern as the dime novel. The
forces of good were pitted against the forces of evil in suitable
Western settings. The heroes were plainsmen or hunters, the
villains Indians, bandits, or Mexicans. The only real difference
between the novels and the plays was the visual appeal of seeing
such events acted out. Often the heroes' roles were played by
those who had actually been there—such men as William Cody,
Wild Bill Hickok, and Texas Jack Omohundro. The villains were
played by stock actors, and the obligatory Indians by people
hired off the street. The audience was always treated to much
gunfire and spectacle (prairie fires, cyclones, and floods were
not unknown), and a horse almost always made an appearance
somewhere in the course of the evening.

These plays were no more true to life than the dime novels
were, but they had a great popularity in the United States and
even made their way to Europe and Australia as the nineteenth
century progressed. Those who saw these plays stored away another set of impressions of the West that added to the total
picture held by Easterners and Europeans alike.

Cody's Wild West show was an immediate success with these
audiences. The dime novel had prepared them for the events
they would see—stagecoach robberies and battles with Indians
were standard fare in the Westerns they had been reading. But
no book, no matter how vividly written, could compete with the
visual spectacle of the colonel's show. For a few short hours the
inhabitants of the cities could smell the gunsmoke, hear the
blood-curdling yells of the Indians, and experience the exciting
events that supposedly made up an average settler's day.

The dime novels and Westerns that Europeans read made no
pretense of being accurate representations of frontier life, and
those who read them knew they were only stories. But the stories
were vivid and exciting and there were thousands of them. Gradually the image of the West that they created superseded all
others in the minds of people all over Europe, and slowly but
surely another part of the myth of the American West was created.

The Wild West, however, did profess to present events and

people as they were on the Plains. Much of the advertising included the words "Everything Genuine." Many newspapers and magazines printed interviews with members of the show who told exciting, real-life stories of their adventures on the Plains. All that the audiences saw and read about the Wild West reinforced the impressions they had gathered from their novels. Like the America Letters and the tales of Western homesteaders, Cody's show was considered true because each member of the audience could see and talk to someone who had actually been west. If a respected Indian scout such as Buffalo Bill said this was how it was, then this was how it was.

The Wild West show was truly a unique entertainment enterprise even if it did draw from other forms. Buffalo Bill's Wild West was related to the circus in its business methods, advertising techniques, and general structure. It was also related to the rodeo because it featured cowboy skills and Western pageantry. But the show was not exclusively a contest between cowboys as is the rodeo; nor was it exclusively a show of exotic animals, death-defying acts, and comic relief as is the circus. Cody blended the excitement and surprise of the circus with demonstrations of Western skills and the narrative of Western melodramas to create the phenomenon of the Wild West show.

Buffalo Bill's show was not the only Wild West company that operated in the late nineteenth and early twentieth century. More than eighty companies have been documented during that period. But Cody's show was the first of this type, the prototype of all Wild Wests and the longest running, most financially successful, most widely traveled, and best-known Wild West that ever performed. Its influence was so great that even the most successful competitors, Pawnee Bill's Wild West, Doc W. F. Carver's Wild America, and the Miller Brothers 101 Ranch Show, ended up copying not only the basic structure of Buffalo Bill's Wild West, but the advertising ideas, program covers, and specific acts. Doc Carver was forced to take his show "around the world" because he couldn't compete with Cody in the United States; the Miller Brothers show saw its biggest success after Buffalo Bill's show was disbanded. Records show that Pawnee Bill's show barely stayed in the black until he joined his Wild West with Cody's in 1909.

The Wild West phenomenon did not disappear when Cody died in 1917. The Miller Brothers 101 Ranch Show continued to tour regularly during the 1920s and sporadically in the 1930s. Other small Wild Wests were begun and retired during the 1930s and 1940s. Many circuses began including a Wild West concert that lasted from 10 to 30 minutes at the end of their programs in the 1920s. This practice continued through the 1930s and 1940s. But after Colonel Cody's death there was never again a single Wild West that enjoyed the huge success and terrific impact of Buffalo Bill's show.

By 1913, when Buffalo Bill lost his show to creditors, the frontier was settled and the myth of the American West was well established. From all the information available to them, all falsified to one degree or another, eastern Americans and Europeans formed a double image of the West. On one hand they saw the frontier as a new Eden, a land of plenty where land was free, hard work rewarded, and people free to do as they liked. On the other hand they saw the frontier as a place of danger and adventure where a person's only friend was a gun, where lawlessness was the rule. These two pictures were neatly blended into one vision by Buffalo Bill's Wild West, and his is the final picture most of us carry in our heads of the Western American frontier.

CHAPTER ONE

HOW TRUTH BECAME FICTION

We hear a great deal about realism on the stage, where a working model of a Westend drawing room is hailed as a triumph of art, but the Buffalo Bill Show is something more than realism—it is reality.[1]

Establishing who first had the idea of creating a Wild West show is next to impossible. These shows developed from several existing forms (such as Indian exhibitions, buffalo hunts, and exhibitions of Western animals) and emerged side by side with other forms (such as circus specs, rodeos, and border dramas) from which they borrowed. But the main problem in trying to resolve this dilemma arises from the number of highly flamboyant people involved with the first productions and from the highly competitive nature of different shows trying to win the same audience. Many people helped develop the original idea, and some claimed credit for more than just improvements. Three men claim to have originated the idea of the Wild West: Doc W. F. Carver, Nate Salsbury, and Colonel W. F. Cody.

Carver's claim can be discounted almost completely. He was Cody's partner during the first season of Wild West touring, and he put up quite a lot of money for this opportunity. That first season was not a great success, and Cody and Carver parted less than amicably. From that time onward, Carver launched a campaign to debunk Cody that included a rival show, lawsuits, and written attacks. During this period his claim of being the originator of the Wild West appeared, and it must be considered in the light of the other absurd claims he was making at the time.

Nate Salsbury also made a written claim to the idea and added that it was he who first thought of using Cody as the star of such a show.[2] What Salsbury actually described was a grand equestrian exhibition with no mention of the Western events that Cody thought so necessary. Salsbury and Cody did discuss a partnership in 1882, but when Cody pulled Doc Carver into the picture, Salsbury withdrew from the project.

Cody's claim consists of actually producing the prototype of a Wild West show as part of a July 4 celebration in 1882 and then organizing his show to tour in the summer of 1883. The idea had many sources, from knowledge of life on the Western plains to Nate Salsbury's suggestions of a large-scale exhibition.

Cody was certainly aware of the many dime novels about Western life that were circulating at the time and was involved in presenting similar stories on the stage. While touring with his melodrama troupe (the Buffalo Bill Combination), he was undoubtedly exposed to other entertainments being offered in the Eastern cities—if for no other reason than keeping an eye on the competition. He would have seen shooting exhibitions, events featuring horsemanship, grand historical spectacles, and perhaps even small groups of Indians being displayed.

Life on the plains also provided Cody with ideas. He had not only his own exciting experiences to draw on, but also his knowledge of roundups, brandings, and other details of life on the ranch. Through his Western adventures Buffalo Bill had become good friends with Wild Bill Hickok, who had been involved in an 1872 scheme that included trying to exhibit buffalo at Niagara Falls. The next season Hickok traveled with the Buffalo Bill Combination, and Cody probably heard the story of this adventure during the tour.

From all of these ideas Cody created a unique and very successful entertainment form.

He learned that it was not fine acting, in the accepted meaning of the phrase, that was most popular with the people. It was the appearance of real Indians, real guides, real scouts, real cowboys, real buffaloes, real bucking horses, and last but not least, real Buffalo Bill, who had already become in the minds of the American people the Ideal American Plainsman.[3]

The prototype of Cody's Wild West was produced in North Platte, Nebraska. The event was called "The Old Glory Blowout" and served as North Platte's Fourth of July celebration in 1882. There are many conflicting accounts of why Cody ended up in charge of producing this event, and it is difficult to determine what really happened. It seems probable that Cody, being the town's only really famous citizen, was asked for advice and saw the perfect opportunity to try out some of his Wild West ideas.

Cody's original idea revolved around two elements: a contest for cowboys and a demonstration of a buffalo hunt. Buffalo Bill himself would pursue a small herd of buffalo around North Platte's fenced race track, but instead of hiring cowboys to demonstrate their skills, Cody persuaded the town to offer prizes for some of the events. The contest was advertised in nearby areas and 1,000 entrants responded.[4] Because these cowboys entered a contest to win prizes instead of being hired as performers, "The Old Glory Blowout" became one of the first recognized rodeos as well as the prototype of the Wild West.

The show was a huge success. Cody hired Indians and old friends to enact events of Western life, ride in the horse races, and demonstrate their abilities with rifle and pistol. People came from miles around to see this unique event. It is fitting that the first Wild West, as well as one of the first rodeos, occurred on the Western plains, the area that Cody would make famous all over the world.

During the theatrical season of 1882–83 Cody directed the organization of his first touring Wild West from the playhouses of the East. He put a good deal of his own money into this enterprise but soon realized that he would need a partner to cover all the expenses. Nate Salsbury claimed that he and Cody had agreed to wait until 1884 to put a show together with the idea that they would tour Europe. But Cody was anxious to begin his show in the summer of 1883 and managed to convince Doc Carver to put money into the project. Salsbury refused to be pushed into a partnership with Carver, since he felt Carver was a fake who knew nothing of either the West or show business. Cody ignored Salsbury's objections to Carver and took him on as a partner. Salsbury withdrew all support for the first season but did not give up on his ideas for an equestrian exhibition.

Carver put up $27,000 to become Cody's sole partner for the first season. There was an immediate argument about the name of the enterprise. Carver held out for "Golden West" while Cody pushed for "Cody and Carver Wild West." The final name that went on the posters and advertisements was "Hon. W. F. Cody and Dr. W. F. Carver's Rocky Mountain and Prairie Exhibition."

The show opened in Omaha, Nebraska, on May 19, 1883, with a cast of characters drawn from all over the West. Both Carver and Cody performed shooting acts in the show, as did Captain A. H. Bogardus and his four sons. Other notables included Major Frank North, in charge of the Pawnee Indians; Gordon Lillie, interpreter; Fred Mathews, stagecoach driver; Buck Taylor, King of the Cowboys; and Johnny Baker, the Cowboy Kid. Also with the show were the black bear "Uno" and his trainer Bronco John.[5]

The program for this opening season was:

1. Grand Introductory March
2. Bareback Pony Race
3. Pony Express
4. Attack on the Deadwood Mail Coach
5. 100 Yard Race between an Indian on foot and an Indian on horseback
6. Capt. A. H. Bogardus
7. Cody and Carver—shooting exhibition
8. Race between Cowboys
9. Cowboy's Fun
10. Riding Wild Texas Steers
11. Roping and Riding Wild Bison
12. Grand Hunt—including a battle with the Indians[6]

While the show did not make either partner rich, the two men did manage to cover expenses and return their show to Omaha at the end of the summer. By this time it was clear that Cody and Carver could not continue as partners. There were disagreements over every aspect of the show. Carver claimed that Cody was continually drunk and that he never did his share of the work. However, observers have stated that Carver was just as unreliable and just as often drunk.[7] In fact, it seems likely that most of the company did as much celebrating as they did performing.

Carver wished to continue the tour through the winter, while Cody was ready for a rest. Carver's biographer, Raymond Thorpe, claims that Carver finally ended the partnership by demanding that the drunken Cody give up all the equipment and stock to pay off a $29,000 debt. Thorpe goes on to say that Cody, afraid that he would lose everything, suggested that the partners flip a coin to determine who retained ownership of each item. According to this biography, Carver won everything except one carload of horses which he promptly bought from Cody.[8]

This account serves to show just how bitter Doc Carver had become by the time he told his life story to Raymond Thorpe. There probably was an incident of coin flipping, since the story appears in many variants throughout the Cody literature. It is even probable that one or both parties were drunk at the time. Thorpe's claim that Doc had initially "purchased the outfit" is false, however. Cody had already gathered together much of the equipment and performers for "The Old Glory Blowout" long before he entered into partnership with Carver. Carver's money was used primarily to cover traveling and operating expenses.

The exact disposition of the assets of the show is not recorded anywhere. But Carver did not win the entire show, since it is known that Cody kept at least the Deadwood Stage. He also retained the loyalty of all the major staff members and most of the star performers who toured with Cody the following year instead of joining Carver's newly formed show.

The season of 1884 marked the beginning of one of the most famous partnerships in all of show business. Cody returned to his original plan and again approached Nate Salsbury with an offer of partnership. Salsbury agreed since Doc Carver was now out of the picture, and Captain Bogardus was added as a third partner. (Bogardus remained with the show only through the 1884 season and seems to have contributed little more than money to the management of the show.) Under the new management the show was rechristened "Buffalo Bill's Wild West, America's

National Entertainment," and began a series of one-a-day stands in the Midwest and East.

This tour was quite different from the wild revels of the year before because Salsbury knew the business of touring. He carefully planned a route, instituted careful bookkeeping, and set down a strict set of rules that ensured a sober cast for each performance. Under his prodding even Cody agreed to give up drinking while on the road.

However, not everything ran as smoothly as it might. Salsbury did not travel with the Wild West during the first season because he was busy managing his traveling acting troupe, the "Troubadour Company." This left Cody in charge of everyday decisions, and he hired an old friend, Pony Bob Haslam, as his advance agent. All went well until the inexperienced Haslam was sent to hire a boat to take the show down the Mississippi River to New Orleans for the World's Industrial and Cotton Exposition, where the show was to play for the winter months. Nate Salsbury later described the results this way:

The immediate cause of all our trouble was the lack of foresight in hiring the boat. She was a "tub" of the tubbiest description, but our talented Bob was more familiar with the merits of a bronco than he was with boats in general, and this one in particular. When our tub reached a place called Rodney she collided with a boat coming up the river, and was so badly damaged that the Captain ran her ashore, where she was patched up, and then she set out again on her journey. She moved out into the stream and went down in thirty feet of water in four minutes.[9]

This version of the incident is quite different from contemporary newspaper accounts. According to both the *Cincinnati Enquirer* and the *New Orleans Picayune* there was a collision of two well-known steamboats, but the boat carrying the Wild West went down in only eight feet of water, and all passengers and stock were unharmed.

Another version of this incident includes an exchange of telegrams between Salsbury and Cody with Cody sending: "Outfit at bottom of river. What do you advise?" And Salsbury replying: "Go to New Orleans, reorganize, and open on your date."[10] This exchange may have taken place, but it seems unlikely, as Cody

was in New Orleans when the boat went down and only jour-
neyed to Rodney's Landing after receiving a telegraph from A.
E. Shible advising him that everything was under control.[11] Cody
did get his group reorganized and moved down the Mississippi
in time to open in New Orleans as he intended.

He might as well have left the show stranded on the sandbar
for all the good the New Orleans stand did the show. It rained
for 44 days straight while the show struggled to survive in mud
and muck and while the audience stayed home. By the end of
the stand at the exposition the show was $60,000 in the red and
its only assets were some horses, "twenty five Indians in the
saddle, seven Mexicans, and eight cowboys."[12] But during those
rainy days in New Orleans Cody also added the biggest star
attraction he ever had. Annie Oakley came to audition and was
hired on the strength of a short exhibition.

The program of events did not change much for the seasons
of 1884–85. The show followed a pattern similar to that of the
first season, but a few more of what were to become the standard
events were added.

The Indians were given an event of their own to exhibit scalp
and war dances; Annie Oakley's act was added; the "Grand Hunt"
became simply Cody hunting buffalo; the "Attack on the Settler's
Cabin" became the closing act; and Cody added the first event
that was a reenactment of an episode in his life—"The Duel with
Yellow Hand." Cody also added Sitting Bull to the program in
1885, and from that season onward he always featured some
famous Indian chief in the Wild West.[13]

The show continued its one-a-day stands through 1885. It
toured the Central and Eastern states early in the summer, then
made a swing into Canada, with Sitting Bull becoming the greatest attraction. The show then returned to the states and finished
the season in Youngstown, Ohio.

During the next two years Buffalo Bill's Wild West made the
transition from a small outdoor touring show to one of the greatest amusement enterprises ever known. This transition was due
to three significant ideas: The idea of playing the Wild West in
long engagements on permanent grounds, the idea of playing
the show as a grand spectacle in Madison Square Garden, and
the idea of taking the Wild West to Europe. Each of these ideas

originated with Nate Salsbury, was capitalized on by the great press agent Major John Burke, and was made the most of in the arena by William F. Cody.

The first long stand of Buffalo Bill's Wild West was made at Erastina, Staten Island, from June to September in 1886. People from New York City mobbed the ferries to Staten Island, and the show began making good profits. Cody sums it up in a letter to his friend Jack Crawford: "My success here has been the greatest ever known in the amusement business, the receipts greater, and New York is wild over the show. I am taking about $40,000 a week—something never heard of before."[14]

The profits earned over that summer made it possible for Cody and Salsbury to consider renting Madison Square Garden for a winter engagement. This enterprise would cost $18,000 per month for the building alone. The partners proposed to hire Steele Mackaye, Matt Morgan, and Nelse Waldron to create the grand spectacle they wished to perform. Steele Mackaye estimated the overall cost for scenery and effects would be $8,500. The final price was actually even greater than this.

Mackaye took the raw material of the Wild West and converted it into a pageant of American pioneer life. In order to achieve his aims, he rebuilt entire sections of Madison Square Garden, helped to invent new scenic effects and machines, and wrote a "scenic scenario of group pantomime, structurally accompanied and interpreted, at strategic points by terse-spoken 'oration,' amplified in tone-volume by a projective sounding-board."[15] He called the new show *The Drama of Civilization*.

Scene painter Matt Morgan was hired to paint the four huge cycloramas (40 feet by 150 feet) and the six straight drops that provided the scenery for the show. A temporary grid had to be built to house the rigging for these drops, and the painting was done mostly from a chair-swing suspended from the garden's roof. The total cost of canvas and paint was $1,280.

While the scenery was being painted, Nelse Waldron was busily organizing the machines needed to effect both a cyclone and a prairie fire on stage. With Mackaye's help four six-foot exhaust fans were rigged to batteries that ran on steam. The steam was obtained by digging trenches across 27th Street to Steven's car shops. When these fans were turned on a set covered with dried leaves, the force of the wind was enough to unseat riders from their horses.

Mackaye spent most of his time trying to coach the performers in their roles. For his pantomimes to have the greatest effect, certain groupings had to be achieved and certain actions taken. Nate Salsbury continually advised Mackaye to set broad outlines and leave the details to the cowboys and Indians. This suggestion made sense because most of the performers were not trained actors, but they had been in situations similar to the ones being depicted. Steele Mackaye apparently struggled for more specific effects than this.

Mr. Mackaye was soon busy holding rehearsal, but the Indians would have discouraged Delsarte himself.... Mr. Mackaye posed and drilled the Indians, the cowboys, the old settlers and the mules in picturesque groups. He tried to get the Old Settler to look as if he was lying when he was telling stories.—Mr. Mackaye was vastly tired, when he got through the day's rehearsal.[16]

Steele Mackaye's efforts paid off. The show was a trememdous success. *The Drama of Civilization* was broken down into four Epochs or acts with Interludes in between. The first Epoch was "The Primeval Forest" and featured both wild animals leased from Adam Forepaugh's circus and Cody's Indians. This Epoch ended with a large battle between Indian tribes. The first Interlude included more Indian dances and the sharpshooting of Miss Lillian Smith.

"The Prairie" was the setting for the second Epoch. Here the buffalo hunt appeared, and an emigrant train was added to the equipment already owned by Cody's show. This Epoch ended with a prairie fire and a huge stampede. The second Interlude allowed the cowboys to show their skills at trick riding, roping, and bronc busting.

The scene then changed to the "Cattle Ranch." This Epoch was designed around Cody's event, "The Attack on the Settler's Cabin," and was filled with gunfire and yelling Indians. The shooting acts of Cody and Annie Oakley followed this Epoch.

Finally the progress of civilization reached the "Mining Camp." This was meant to be the big finale, and the Epoch was broken down into three scenes. The first scene included a Pony Express event and some of the specialty acts of the cowboys. It also allowed for a classic gunfight in the street (the only time such an event was included in Cody's show). The second scene occurred in a canyon and showed the Deadwood Stage being attacked by bandits. Finally, the scene returned to the mining camp, and the cyclone struck, destroying all in its path.

To this already ambitious program a fifth Epoch was added: the reenactment of Custer's Last Stand, complete with a cyclorama painting of the valley of the Little Big Horn. It is not clear if this event was a part of the original plan or not, because it was not included in the early performances. But later reviews talk of little else. It starred Buck Taylor as the famous general, and the battle raged until the last soldier was killed. After a moment of silence in which the audience could take in the tableau, Cody would gallop into the arena at the head of his cowboy band, react to the battlefield scene, and doff his hat in respect for the dead. At this point he would be picked up by a spotlight, the arena lights would be lowered, and a projection of the words "Too late!" would be flashed on a screen behind him.

Percy Mackaye makes repeated claims that it was his father who gave shape and dramatic interest to a loosely formed and chaotic program. It is his contention that it was his father's ideas and direction that made the show a successful and famous enterprise. A careful study of the program for *The Drama of Civilization* as well as the Wild West programs preceding and following it reveals that Mackaye's influence was less important than this, although his ideas did have some effect on the show.

Some of Mackaye's additions were impossible to perform in the outdoor arenas that were the Wild West's usual performance space. Among these were both the prairie fire and the cyclone, though both were revived for indoor performances in England the following winter. The scene in the Primeval Forest also proved unsatisfactory, since the Plains Indians featured by Buffalo Bill did not live this way, and Cody balked at presenting anything this far from the genuine situation.

Many of the other events that appeared in *The Drama of Civilization* had been lifted directly from events already traditional in Wild West performances. There was nothing new in the Pony

Express, the attack on a ranch by Indians, or a buffalo hunt. Even Mackaye could see the theatrical worth of the sharpshooting acts and "Cowboy Fun," and he broke his chronological order to give them space in his pageant.

Using a chronological progression was a unique and useful idea for the production Mackaye created, but it had little use without the grand climactic effects and the amazing scenery possible in Madison Square Garden. Cody had limited resources in the open arena and had little or no way to tie events together into a dramatic whole. He knew how to build audience interest by using the order of events that had worked for him in the past, and he stuck with that order. The Epochs were repeated as written by Mackaye only during the Manchester engagement the following winter.

However, Mackaye did make some important contributions. The first was his idea of using an orator. From the Madison Square Garden engagement on, Cody was never without an announcer. He had to experiment to find the correct placement and manner of voice amplification, but he knew a good idea when he saw one.

Two new events also made their first appearance in *The Drama of Civilization*. Both the emigrant train and the reenactment of an Indian battle became standard events in the Wild West. The Custer battle was revived in one form or another during many seasons between 1884 and 1913. The idea of using covered wagons was put to use immediately and never again left the program. Whether these ideas came exclusively from Steele Mackaye or were the result of collaboration with Salsbury and Cody, it was Mackaye who first made them work, and Cody who saw their value and made use of them year after year.

In the spring of 1887 Cody and Salsbury incorporated the Wild West and chartered the steamship *State of Nebraska* to take their show to England. Salsbury had had this trip in mind from the very beginning. With his great enthusiasm and energy he convinced Cody that the difficulties of moving the show over such a great distance could be solved and then set out to see that they were.

The loading of the ship itself in late March apparently was quite a sight. The Deadwood Stage and other equipment were loaded over the side with little trouble, but the livestock was a different matter. The horses, donkeys, deer, and elk all struggled and panicked.

The buffalo went over without a murmur, though almost scared to death. The people who watched the transfer from the shore made the interesting discovery that a horned buffalo being yanked over the ship's side in a sling, hanging up by the middle with head and heels together, is a much more comical sight than anything in the show itself, and they laughed until their sides ached, though the buffalo didn't seem to find it amusing.[17]

Once the animals and equipment were loaded, the Indians, cowboys, sharpshooters, and other personnel were settled in their accommodations. The *State of Nebraska* set sail on March 31, 1887, to the accompaniment of the newly added Cowboy Band playing "The Girl I Left Behind Me."

The crossing was quite rough, and the performers and stock suffered badly from seasickness. Upon the ship's arrival on April 18, the cattle and buffalo were subjected to quarantine, and the ammunition for the show's sharpshooters was banned. The quarantine was a short one, however, and the ammunition was merely stored by the British army and issued as needed.[18] The company rallied after these difficulties, and all pitched in to finish the grandstands and establish their camp at Earl's Court, Kensington, so that they could be ready to help Queen Victoria celebrate her Jubilee.

Reporters, nobles, and commoners alike besieged the members of the company wherever they went. Edward, Prince of Wales, asked for a preview showing, a favor that was quickly granted. The prince became the Wild West's greatest fan as a result of this performance. His patronage did wonders for the advertising of the show in a land where royal activities were closely watched.

The Wild West gave its first official London performance on May 9, 1887, to a packed house. This triumph was followed by a performance for Queen Victoria on May 11. The Queen had attended almost no public entertainments since the death of the Prince Consort 25 years before, so her visit to the Wild West was considered an event indeed. She set down the stipulation that all must be concluded in one hour (though she stayed for the extra fifteen minutes that were required to see the whole program), and she decreed that the program must begin promptly at five o'clock.

The arrangements made quite an impression on one cowboy:

For four blocks around where we was showin' there was soldiers...the Coldstream Guards, I think they was. They sure looked like giants, every man jack of 'em standin' six foot, and on their heads they all wore these here busbies, and that added about two feet to each man.... The soldiers were placed side by side so close their shoulders was touchin'. They made a sort of human fence, and it would have been impossible for anyone to get past that fence, or for anyone to get out either.[19]

The Queen liked the Wild West so well that she arranged for another command performance on June 20. This performance was attended by royal guests of the Queen from all over Europe.

The Wild West impressed not only its royal audience, but its everyday audiences as well. From May through October the show played to 30,000 or 40,000 people a day on the grounds at Earl's Court. Cody and Salsbury then took their show to Birmingham and finally to a winter stand in Manchester. Played inside, the Manchester engagement was closely based on *The Drama of Civilization* and used much of the same scenery and machinery. This pageant was not as popular as the outdoor show, and the *Persian Monarch* was chartered to take the Wild West home to New York in the spring of 1888.

The 1888 season was a return engagement at Staten Island, and American audiences were even more enthusiastic about "America's National Entertainment" than they had been in 1886. Major Burke, Cody's press agent, made great use of the acclaim the show had received in England, and American audiences gladly welcomed the heroes home.

The program of events was still evolving during this period. Cody and Annie Oakley had argued during the London engagement, and she did not return to Staten Island with the show. There were many standard acts still featured, including "The Pony Express," "The Buffalo Hunt," and "The Deadwood Stage," but the show was still trying to find the right combination of sharpshooting, trick riding, and racing events to link the more theatrical acts together. The addition of an orator and musical accompaniment from William Sweeney's Cowboy Band helped to provide continuity, and the show was beginning to take on the form that proved most successful with the public.

Cody had discovered how to open and close his show effectively. He began with a review of the performers, arranged in groups. Then Buffalo Bill would gallop in, introduce the company, and start them off into a grand serpentine salute that ended with his own exit. The final salute or bow by the entire company had become standard during the London performances.

Salsbury was not satisfied with his conquest of England. He wanted to conquer the continent as well. To achieve this end, he arranged for the Wild West to appear in Paris as part of the *Exposition Universale* in 1889. The show sailed on the *Persian Monarch* once again and was not to return to the States until 1893.

The show was well attended, and all things Western became the fad. All sorts of curios and dime novels were sold on the grounds, and popcorn was introduced to Parisian audiences. The show's performers took advantage of the opportunity to see the sights, and Major Burke took advantage of the opportunity to have the performers seen sightseeing by reporters and potential audience members alike. The Indians were taken up the Eiffel Tower in full regalia, the cowboys wandered the streets in Stetsons and boots, and Cody and Salsbury attended parties and shows.

After a six-month stand in Paris the Wild West began a tour of the European continent that was composed mostly of one-a-day stands with longer stays in larger cities. First they traveled through southern France, then into Spain where influenza and unappreciative audiences nearly finished the show. Once free of Spain, they traveled to Italy and Germany, where they set up camp for the winter. Enthusiastic audiences greeted the show in every town, and money poured into the box office. Salsbury and Cody were fast becoming rich men.

There was a growing problem, however. An Indian named

White Horse left the show somewhere in Europe and made his way back to the United States in the hold of a freighter. There is no evidence to suggest why he left the show beyond the story he told to the *New York Herald* of starvation and cruelty at Cody's hands. He told the newspaper that "all the Indians in Buffalo Bill's show are discontented, ill-treated, and anxious to come back home. Food and clothing are scarce, and Rocky Bear, the chief, and Broncho Bill, the interpreter, are cruel in their treatment of the Indians."[20] The printed story caused quite a disturbance, not only because of concern for the Indians still with Cody, but because of the effect such a report might have on reservation Indians already stirred up by the Ghost Shirt movement. Cody replied in another *Herald* article saying, "After leaving Paris, in order to reduce expenses for our tour of the provinces, some of the Indians were sent back to the reservation. Since the show went into winter quarters the remainder were sent home, and every man, woman, and child wants to be employed by us next season."[21] It was obvious that the show must be cleared of all allegations if it were to continue, because the Wild West had to have government permission to recruit Indians at the beginning of each season, and without Indians the Wild West would not be much of a show. Salsbury quickly moved to forestall further problems. He invited the German embassy officials to tour his facility and examine the Indians on the grounds. After receiving their unqualified praise for the care the Indians were given, he sent Cody and the Indians to Washington for further inspection. Cody quickly concluded his business in Washington, where an official of the Bureau of Indian Affairs examined the Indians and cleared Cody of all allegations of mistreatment. Because of the evidence of the German embassy officials and the bureau's own investigation, Cody was allowed to return the Indians to the reservation and recruit new Indians to return to Europe with him. It was decided that the case of White Horse was isolated and exaggerated, and the matter was dropped.

Cody then was called to the Standing Rock Reservation by General Miles to help convince Sitting Bull to surrender to the U.S. Army. Cody did what he could in this affair but was unsuccessful, and Sitting Bull was shot. This brought about the exodus of a large band of Sioux from the reservation and eventually led to the Wounded Knee Massacre.

Cody was not present at Wounded Knee though he was serving as a brigadier general in the Nebraska National Guard during the conflict. His main mission seems to have been to help keep the conflict from erupting into another Indian war. He went to the Pine Ridge Agency and was present when peace was announced. After this brief return to army life, Cody returned to Europe, taking with him a full contingent of Indians, including nineteen prisoners of war from the Wounded Knee conflict.

During Cody's absence, Salsbury had begun to implement his idea of including an exhibition of horsemanship in the Wild West. He wanted to be sure there was a show if Cody returned without the Indians, and he knew that new events would help to attract larger audiences even if the Indians did return. With all this in mind, he hired twenty German soldiers, twenty English soldiers, twenty U.S. soldiers, and twelve Cossacks to exhibit military and riding skills. With these additions the entire company numbered 640 in the spring of 1891.[22]

This new company traveled through Germany, Belgium, and on to England that year. By the time they reached England, they had also added six Argentine Gauchos to their number. In 1892 they traveled in Scotland, Ireland, and finally returned to London for the summer season. On October 14, 1892, they sailed for home on the *Mohawk*.

The season of 1893 was to be the most successful ever played by the Wild West. In this year Chicago hosted the World's Columbian Exposition. Salsbury did not manage to win space on the grounds for his show, but he did manage the next best thing. He rented a lot directly across the street from the main entrance to the exposition. The show also boasted a new name, "Buffalo Bill's Wild West and Congress of Rough Riders of the World," and a number of events that audiences in the U.S. had not seen. Futhermore, the show had not played anywhere but New York for six years before the Chicago showing, and Cody's success in Europe was well-known in the United States.

The show played to packed houses all summer. The World's Fair drew huge crowds to Chicago, and Buffalo Bill's show was easily accessible to these visitors. Profits for this one summer have been estimated at between $700,000 and $1,000,000.[23] Salsbury and Cody had finally found the successful combination of theatrical and spectacular events that would carry their show to fame and fortune.

Back in New York for the season of 1894, the Wild West did less well. In fact, this season at Ambrose Park made it clear that long stands were no longer a lucrative idea. On top of the strain of a poor season, Nate Salsbury became ill in 1894. To fill the gap caused by his absence from active management, Salsbury and Cody signed an agreement with James Bailey of the Barnum and Bailey Circus. Bailey was to provide transportation and touring expenses in return for a share in the profits.

Bailey's influence was immediately felt. Using standard circus practice, he routed the show through a series of one-a-day stands for the 1895 season that covered 131 stands in 190 days with 9,000 miles of travel.[24] This basic formula was followed for the next six years.

Following another circus tradition, Bailey added a side show to the Wild West in 1902. The show had always had a midway where audience members could purchase souvenirs, drinks, popcorn, and the like, but there had never been side show performers associated with the Wild West before this date.

While this type of touring brought in substantial profits and made Cody the best-known figure in America, it took its toll. Cody was in his mid-fifties by the time those six years of grueling traveling were over. His letters suggest that he was tired and unhappy and always in financial difficulties. He invested his money in many projects but was never able to oversee their implementation because of his travels. Con artists and friends alike took advantage of his generosity, and while his show continued to enjoy popularity, his vitality and fortunes began to ebb.

The show itself stayed nearly the same during these years, but a new element did begin to appear. Each year some great military battle was reenacted as a part of the show. In the early years this battle had been Custer's Last Stand. But as the Spanish-American War and the Boxer Rebellion took on increasing importance, the Indian battles disappeared and more recent battles were included. "The Battle of San Juan Hill" was a favorite, as was "The Battle of Tien-Tsin." As part of this increased emphasis on military prowess, other events were also added. These included artillery drills, life-saving drills, and cavalry drills.

Buffalo Bill's show returned to Europe in 1902. This was arranged as a swap of equipment and territory between the Barnum and Bailey Circus, which had been touring in Europe since 1897, and the Wild West, which had been touring America during this period. This move on Bailey's part probably kept both shows alive, as they did not have to compete with each other for audiences, but it must also be noted that Cody's show was not returned to its native land for five years. If the switch was good for both businesses, why wasn't it ever tried again?

Salsbury helped plan the move to Europe and was responsible for booking the show into the Olympia Theatre for its first date. He even planned to accompany the show to London to get it off to a good start but was too ill to make the trip. He died on December 24, 1902, just two days before the show was to open in London.

Nate Salsbury's influence on the Wild West should not be underestimated. He organized it so effectively that it overcame many difficulties with relative ease. He routed the Wild West with such care that there was always an enthusiastic crowd awaiting the performers—whether in America or Europe. But most important, he was able to fuse his ideas with Cody's in such a way that each major change occurred smoothly and successfully. "Nate Salsbury possessed the genius necessary to remaining in the background and letting the public devote its entire interest to the man who formed the romance of the establishment, Buffalo Bill."[25] But his subtle guidance would be sorely missed. The vision of a Wild West show featuring events from American pioneer life and feats of horsemanship that he and Cody had shared for twenty years was soon to become faded and mixed with the world of the circus.

The tour of Europe that had begun so tragically with Salsbury's death continued to be plagued by disaster. The weather was not good, Cody was thrown from a horse and had to appear in a buggy for six weeks, 200 horses had to be destroyed when glanders (a highly contagious, often fatal respiratory disease in horses) broke out in France, and in the final year of the tour, James Bailey died.

Cody was deeply in debt when he returned for his 1907 season, which began in Madison Square Garden. He had continually invested his earnings in business projects that brought little return, never setting aside the cash that would be needed to winter the Wild West and get it on the road again in the spring. In order to keep all his ready cash invested in his business interests, he constantly had to borrow money from his partners to keep the show moving. He had sold two-thirds of his show to Bailey and taken out an additional note with him for $12,000.[26] Cody claimed that he had paid off the $12,000, but he had no receipt to prove his claim. The Bailey estate insisted on payment, and Buffalo Bill had to find the money somewhere. He mortgaged his property and borrowed from friends, knowing that money would begin pouring in as soon as the show began its tour.

Beginning in 1907, Cody began to strip away some of the acts that Bailey had introduced and replace them with more strictly Western events. He removed "The Battle of San Juan Hill" and put in "The Battle of Summit Springs" (an Indian battle in which he had been a scout). Cody also added a game of football on horseback between Indians and cowboys and a new event called "The Great Train Holdup." The final spectacle was changed to "A Holiday at TE Ranch." (The TE was Cody's ranch in the Big Horn Basin of Wyoming.) Audiences no longer saw battles from the latest war or repeated events emphasizing military preparedness. Instead they viewed approximately twenty separate events, of which only three were not explicitly Western in theme.

Buffalo Bill coped quite well with the demands of management. He rented the physical equipment of the show from the Ringling Brothers at $25,000 a year. He arranged to share the Ringling Brothers and Barnum and Bailey winter quarters for another rental fee.[27] Then he arranged two years of touring for his troupe. The established pattern of one-a-day stands was followed, and the show brought in enough money to cover its expenses and pay regular salaries to all the personnel. Although Cody remained in debt to the Bailey estate, no new financial problems arose, and Buffalo Bill's Wild West and Congress of Rough Riders of the World continued to be seen all over America.

But Cody could not continue to walk this tightrope for long. He needed a partner to provide financial backing over the long term if he was ever going to clear his show of debt and retire comfortably. This partner appeared in the person of Gordon W. Lillie, known in Wild West circles as Pawnee Bill.

Lillie had begun his show career as Cody's interpreter in 1884. From that experience he moved on to mount his own show in 1888. His first effort at competing with the Buffalo Bill show ended in disaster, as Cody waged a vicious billposting war and advertising campaign to remove Pawnee Bill from the picture. Lillie eventually lost his show and returned to his home state of Oklahoma, but he did not lose his desire to have a show of his own. In 1890 Lillie again put a Wild West on tour, and this time he was more successful. The Buffalo Bill show was in Europe for seven of the seventeen years the two shows competed, and during two other years Cody was playing long stands in one location, while Pawnee Bill toured his show. While Cody played Ambrose Park in Brooklyn during 1894, Pawnee Bill toured Belgium and France. The Pawnee Bill Show saw as many financial ups and downs over the years as any other outdoor amusement enterprise, but at the end of each season it was always clear that there would be another season to follow.

Pawnee Bill may have felt some satisfaction in saving a show that had ruined his own, but he also knew a good gamble when he saw one. It was obvious that Cody had a huge following all over America, and equally obvious that Buffalo Bill knew how to dazzle a crowd with carefully planned arena spectacle. Merging the two shows would not be terribly difficult, as they both followed a similar pattern. The best cowboys, Indians, and other types of performers could be chosen from each group to make up the company for the next season. The same procedure could be followed with the equipment and stock.

Gordon Lillie took the gamble and purchased the two-thirds interest held by the Bailey estate, as well as the equipment from the Ringlings in 1908. He offered Buffalo Bill a chance to recover a half interest in the show from his share of the profits to come. By the end of 1911 the show was successful enough to allow Cody to seize this chance.

The newly formed show took on a new name and a slightly altered program. Officially called "Buffalo Bill's Wild West and Pawnee Bill's Far East," it was known in most places as the Two

Bills Show. Pawnee Bill instituted only one major change in the program, but it was an important one. In every program an event called "The Far East or A Dream of the Orient" was performed. This act included dancing elephants, camels, and "an ethnological congress of strange tribes, clans, races, and nations of peculiar people."[28] Based largely on circus spectaculars, the Far East took about fifteen minutes to perform. Combined with the side show added to the Wild West by Bailey and never removed, the Far East brought the show closer to being a circus than Cody ever dreamed it would get.

In 1910 the two partners began a series of Farewell Tours. Cody had announced his intention of retiring, and people flocked to see the show. Profits of $800,000 were realized in the next two years, meaning that Cody received $400,000 as his share.[29] Most, if not all, of the profits Cody realized from the show were pumped into a mine that Cody had bought in Arizona. The mine was never very profitable, and it took every penny Cody could scrape together to keep it running. But Cody also desperately wanted to own his half of the show again, so he sold his North Platte ranch to Lillie for $100,000. Cody's wife Lulu received $80,000 and Lillie the other $20,000. The final $10,000 needed to pay off his Wild West debts was obtained by mortgaging his hotel in Cody, Wyoming, again to Lillie. Pawnee Bill was a rich man at the end of the 1911 season, but Cody had nothing but his half share in the show and his mortgaged properties.

The 1911 season brought in only $125,000. The Wild West was plagued by bad weather and disgruntled audiences. People who had already paid to see Buffalo Bill for the last time felt cheated and betrayed by a man who was supposed to be honest and upright. These audiences did not understand that a man who had made millions of dollars during his career needed to work to pay off his enormous debts.

True to his usual pattern, Cody did not have the $20,000 needed to pay his share of winter expenses in 1912. He set out to borrow the money. While in Denver visiting one of his sisters he met with Harry Tammen, part owner of the *Denver Post* and the Sells-Floto Circus. Tammen was more than willing to loan

Cody the money on a six-month note at 6 percent interest, and Cody was more than willing to sign the note. That signing was the beginning of the end for Buffalo Bill's Wild West.

Tammen was anxious to keep his circus on the road regardless of competition from the gigantic Ringling Brothers Circus Trust. He saw an alliance with Cody as the way to achieve his goals, so he printed a story in the *Denver Post* announcing a merger between the Sells-Floto Circus and the Buffalo Bill Wild West and Pawnee Bill Far East for the 1914 season. A 1913 contract signed by Cody, in which he agreed to travel with the Sells-Floto Circus and manage a Wild West feature for the season of 1914, does exist.[30] This contract gave Tammen exclusive rights to the name "Buffalo Bill." It is not clear if Buffalo Bill signed this agreement thinking it was a part of the loan papers and not actually realizing its content, or if he signed it fully realizing that he was giving up not only ownership of his show but the use of his name. The former seems more likely, since the first two pages of the contract (the ones dealing with the merger and the use of the Buffalo Bill title) are not initialed as are the others and because it seems unlikely that Cody would have relinquished so easily what he had struggled so hard to keep.

Lillie was justifiably furious about the announcement of the merger and became convinced that he had been double-crossed. He agreed to go on with the 1913 season, but he refused to pay any of Cody's share of the show's expenses. If 1913 had been a profitable year, Cody probably could have escaped Tammen's trap, but bad weather and bad routing caused a ruinous season. Money was pouring out, but no profits were coming in. Not only were debts mounting for show expenses, but Cody had no way of gathering together the money to pay off Tammen.

The final blow came when Lillie booked the show into Denver only a few days before Cody's note was due. Why Lillie took this action is not clear. He knew that Tammen controlled the printing company that was waiting for $60,000 owed them by the Two Bills Show for the season's posters and programs, and that Tammen was going to see to it that the show was sued for that amount as soon as it entered Denver. But Lillie took the show into Denver in spite of this knowledge. Perhaps he wished to teach Cody a lesson or perhaps he thought he could trade Cody and his name for the rest of the show. But neither of these things came to pass.

The show was attached in May 1913. Lillie tried to file for bankruptcy, but a further debt was dredged up by Tammen, and Cody was forced to dissolve the partnership. Then Tammen attached the show for nonpayment of the $20,000 note Cody had signed to winter the show, and the Two Bills Show was finished.

The Wild West was auctioned on September 15, 1913, and friends of Cody bought his white horse, Isham, as a gift. The rest of the equipment and stock were sold and the performers stranded without their pay for the season. Cody did what he could to get them enough money to return home, though some simply had to make their own way out of Denver.

Cody returned to his ranch in the Big Horn Basin for the summer and began to plan for his future. While he was tired and feeling old, he was not beaten. His first scheme was to film a series of events from his life with as many of the original characters as possible. This inclination probably came from two sources. The promise of "everything genuine" had long been a major tenet of the Wild West and one Cody believed in absolutely. But just as important was Cody's wish to help his friends by providing them with employment while they provided him with memories of the days of his youth.

With financial backing from Harry Tammen and permission from the Interior Department to use reservation Indians, Cody began filming "The Battle of Wounded Knee." This was one of eight one-reel subjects made by "The Colonel W. F. Cody (Buffalo Bill) Historical Pictures Company."[31] Only fragments and a few complete films still survive in private collections.

Once the filming was complete, Cody traveled with the Sells-Floto Circus to meet his obligations to Tammen. He appeared only to introduce the show and spent most of his time participating in promotional activities set up by the Sells-Floto press agent. He worked on a salary basis, although he got 10 percent of profits over $3,000. The show took a toll on Cody's health, leaving him weak and ill by the end of the season. Nonetheless, he agreed to tour another season. The decision was a difficult one, but he was still deeply in debt and full of new ideas that would require capital.

Touring with the Sells-Floto Circus in 1915 was the worst experience of Cody's show career. The weather was terrible, and Tammen began trying to dupe the audience with false advertising and higher prices. The equipment had been allowed to run down and the main tent was unsafe. Buffalo Bill rebelled and threatened to leave the show if matters were not straightened out.

Using the threat of the original $20,000 debt, Tammen tried to bully Cody into staying with the show. Tammen claimed that the other creditors had received all the proceeds of the auction and that Cody still owed him the entire amount. Tammen announced that he would begin taking money from Cody's salary to satisfy the debt. But Tammen had underestimated Buffalo Bill's reaction to such a move.

Cody's anger frightened Tammen, but Cody forced a face-to-face encounter in Lawrence, Kansas, by flatly refusing to continue the tour until all matters were settled on paper. Once Tammen arrived, it was agreed that Cody would finish the season if all threats against his salary were dropped. The matter of the $20,000 was left unsettled, but by the end of the tour, the show owed Cody $18,000 on his percentage of the profits which he never collected. The debt was canceled in this way, although Tammen continued to try to collect the money through the Denver District Court during 1916.[32]

During the winter of 1915–16 Cody was again thinking up schemes for making money. His idea was to stage a spectacle that would encourage military preparedness, complete with enlistment stations, as part of a Wild West. He got permission from the chief of staff and the promise of soldiers and equipment to make the pageant work. The next step was to find a Wild West that was sufficiently well-known to be able to afford the services of Buffalo Bill. Cody's choice was the "101 Ranch Wild West," and they in turn were anxious to have Cody appear with them. He negotiated a contract that guaranteed him $100 per week and one-third of the profits over $2,750 daily.[33]

The season of 1916 was one of ups and downs for Cody. Early

on, he was making enough money to feel comfortable about his debts and responsibilities. But when attendance dropped and rain and humid heat struck in mid-summer, his health again began to fail, and he became desperate for more money. When the season closed on November 4, he was exhausted and soon contracted a serious cold.

William Cody never recovered from that cold, although he tried hot bath treatments at Glenwood Springs, Colorado, and fought valiantly to recover. When he realized he was dying, he asked to be baptized and confirmed by the Roman Catholic Church. This was done on January 9, 1917. On January 10, Cody died in bed at his sister's house in Denver, Colorado. After his body had lain in state for an entire day in the rotunda of Colorado's state capitol building, Buffalo Bill's coffin was placed in a crypt until spring. As soon as the road was open in the spring, the body was moved from this crypt to Cody's grave on Lookout Mountain, where a funeral service full of pomp and circumstance was held on June 3, 1917. This final resting place was not the one he had chosen—he wished to be buried in Cody, Wyoming—but he had left no money for the huge funeral he deserved and the public demanded, and his wife was forced to accept the best offer made to her. It is truly ironic that it was Harry Tammen and the *Denver Post* who provided the money to bury Cody so far from the place of his choice.

Colonel W. F. Cody's final years were sad indeed. He struggled against huge financial debts and failing health, while trying desperately to maintain his dignity, pride, and reputation for honesty. But these years must be viewed as only a small part of a remarkable life. For most of his 72 years Buffalo Bill was able to live a life of freedom and excitement. He was a part of nearly every important phase of the winning of the West and then proceeded to create a new entertainment enterprise that took that Western experience to people all over the world. Even in his final years he was successful in maintaining his pride and dignity by doing his job with conviction and style. His name is still remembered and the memory of his show continues to bring great pleasure to those who saw it in their youth.

CHAPTER TWO

GETTING THE SHOW ON THE ROAD

Now, a Wild West show in bad weather, it's hell, and when the weather is good, why it's beautiful. So we have good, bad, and indifferent. And then plain hell. Because when it's raining and snowing and the lot is all nothing but mud, why you're riding a buckin' horse there or anything, and you happen to fall in the mud and roll around, why by the time you got to the back end you wouldn't know your outfit.[1]

THE GROUNDS

Buffalo Bill's Wild West toured the eastern United States and Canada, rain or shine, during the seasons of 1884 and 1885. These tours were made in a train of eighteen cars[2] and aboard a Mississippi steamboat that was abandoned at Rodney's Landing. The show was still fairly small (about 300 people), and performances were given in baseball fields, race tracks, and driving parks that already had some seating. To these seats were added bleachers as needed. The space required for the entire layout was not great; however, feeding and housing the company did require careful planning and hard work. The basic system was developed from circus and melodrama touring with special additions made to accommodate the unique personnel and equipment of the Wild West.

Touring proved expensive and exhausting for a group this much larger than a melodrama troupe, and Nate Salsbury instituted the idea of the long run in 1886. He would rent a large piece of ground near a big city, usually New York, and the Wild West would set up a semipermanent camp there, staying four to six months. The population of the city would provide a reliable audience, and these long runs certainly made the trouping life more pleasant. The grandstands were permanent structures built by "construction engineers," and the arena was the same size and shape for every performance. Even the dust and mud in these arenas could be controlled: a detail was regularly assigned to sprinkle the arena with water during dry times, and tile drains were installed to carry off rain water in wet times.

The scenery could be more elaborate than that used when touring because it could be built permanently into the arena. Rocks and trees could be placed in front of the backdrop to provide cover for Indians and cowboys alike, and recognized scenic artists could be hired with money that might otherwise have been spent on touring expenses.

The camp was also more pleasant, because tents could be pitched on grass, paths could be graveled, fences constructed, and flowers grown. These grounds became home for the company during their run and were often left for the community to use when the show closed.

Sometimes the Wild West would perform in structures that had been built for other purposes. They performed in Madison Square Garden in New York; the Great Hall and Skating Rink in Birmingham, the Hippodrome in Manchester, the Olympia Theatre in London; they even gave an exhibition in the Colosseum in Rome. These performances usually involved even more elaborate scenery and effects, as time and money did not have to be spent on tents and the grandstand. Most of these spaces were indoors as well, which provided protection for large painted drops and delicate machinery. During these stands the company was usually quartered in rented rooms or hotels, although the show train was sometimes near enough to be used for this purpose.

But Buffalo Bill was not able to bring in enough money to pay his huge overhead with the long stands, so the show was taken on the road once more. From 1905 until 1913, the Wild West played mostly one-day stands. A system had to be developed for scheduling, booking, moving, and performing the show. The system used during the first years of the show had to be adapted to deal with a much larger, self-contained unit, and suitable show lots had to be discovered in every new town and city. Many of the procedures for moving and setting up the show were taken directly from common circus practices of the day. With James Bailey as a partner these procedures were easily learned and implemented.

Selecting a site for the Wild West grounds was a complicated process. There were many factors to be considered and little time to accomplish the task. First and foremost the grounds had to be accessible to the public, for without an audience there was no show. But the grounds also needed to be in a place with ready access to the railroad, either adjacent to the line or near a road-way that led to the tracks. The closer the grounds were to the railroad, the less time it took to move the show to and from the lot, and an hour saved meant a great deal to people who worked sixteen hours a day, six days a week. Besides these two important requirements, the lot needed to be supplied with fresh water, either from the city supply or from a river or stream.

The size of the grounds also had to be considered. The lot needed to encompass eleven acres to provide room for an arena at least 150 feet wide by 320 feet long (preferably level and smooth), seating for up to 15,000 people, backstage space at least large enough for the Deadwood Stage and a six-mule hitch, living and dining quarters for as many as 700 people, stabling for 500 horses and 18 buffalo, and room for ticket wagons, a blacksmith tent, a barber's tent, the side show annex, and food and trinket concessions. The less tightly packed together all of these things were, the more audience members could wander the grounds and the more money could be made. These size requirements usually meant that the show grounds had to be on the outskirts of town because there rarely was a space that was large enough within the city limits.

Once the site was chosen, rental and licensing fees were paid, and if the grounds were satisfactory the first time they were used, the Wild West usually returned year after year. All this searching and selecting was done by the Wild West's advance men. They settled the question of where the show would play; it was up to the rest of the company to set up the arena and camp and give a crowd-pleasing performance.

The Wild West did not travel with a circus big top because the shooting acts would have made short work of such a canvas canopy. But they did have canvas to cover the grandstand, and all of the living and dining quarters were basic canvas tents. The Wild West traveled with a full complement of roustabouts to rig this canvas and construct the grandstand.

The grandstand was put up by four teams. First, the canvas-men put up the grandstand canvas. Then the seat teams took over. One team put up the section of the regular admission seats (blue seats) closest to the reserved seats (the "front end"). A second team put up the blue seats farthest from the reserved seats (the "back end"). The third team put up the reserved seats. Each team had eighteen men, and every man had a specific duty.

Each team had a superintendent and an assistant who marked out the exact positions for the seating and made sure the assembly was correctly completed. The toe levelers made certain that the sections of seats were level on the vertical plane while the plank levelers made certain that each seat was level on the horizontal plane. Once they were level, the stair-step risers were held in place by the stringer-setters. Then the stringers were pegged in place by the toe-pin setters and drivers at the low end, while the jack setters placed A-frame pieces along the length of the stringers to support them. Then the riser was again checked for level and blocked up if necessary by the block boy.

Once two adjacent stringers were in place, the plank-up men laid the seat planks across the frames and the final leveling was accomplished by the block boy. As each section was completed the side-wall men hung pieces of canvas across the back of the seats to prevent people from seeing the show through the grand-stand without paying.[3]

All around this central effort, other teams were quickly putting up the living and dining quarters and positioning the ticket wagons and props. (The general outline of the camp can be seen in Figure 1.)

The general staff and the performers were housed two to a tent during a long run. Each tent was twelve feet square and contained a bed, a table, and special traveling boxes that held the performer's personal belongings.[4] The star performers, own-ers, and long-time management people each had a separate tent that was furnished as they pleased.

The arrangements for dining seem to have varied over the years. The diagram provided shows only one tent, and Luther

Standing Bear mentions only one in his remembrances of the show.[5] But other accounts refer to two tents—one for Indians and Cossacks and one for all other personnel.[6] Whether there was one tent or two, the basic procedure was the same. Each member of the company was issued tickets for the meals to which he was entitled according to his or her contract. A ticket was presented at the door, and the company member then took a place at one of the long tables inside. Each table was covered with a tablecloth and had its own waiters and coffee boy. Once the meal was finished, the dish washers washed the dishes and silverware, and after dinner, they packed it all up for transport to the next stand.

Two other tents were of particular value to the Wild West. One was the blacksmith tent where horses were shod and machinery was repaired. Two smiths and two shoers were kept busy full-time meeting the demands of such a huge show. The other was the dressing tent:

In this big tent the scene was not only typical of the showman's life in general, but was peculiarly a feature of the Wild West Aggregation. In the center of the tent, whose canvas walls were raised a bit from the ground, there was a big tub of water, at which everyone drank. At the side were two others, at which everyone so accustomed washed. Around this trunks, boxes, small bits of widely distributed wardrobe, straw, and army accoutrements littered the earth in picturesque disarray. Nearer the outside walls a rope circled the interior of the tent. On this were hung the varied garments of the performers, which formed the semi-screen behind which they dressed.[7]

Another section of canvas had to be mounted for each performance, providing the scenery or backdrop that filled the open end of the arena. This scenery served to provide a background for the action, and to screen backstage preparations and activities. When the Wild West was on tour, it was not possible to use the huge backdrops that had appeared in their long stands. Photographs confirm that the touring backdrop was sketchily painted canvas sheets that were hung between poles in the same manner that the sidewalls of the grandstand were rigged. There were two walls of canvas, one set up about six feet behind the other. The center section of the front wall was hung on a wire line so the whole section could be pulled off to one side to allow the entrance and exit of large groups of horsemen or large property pieces. When this "curtain" was open, the audience saw the scenery painted on the second wall of canvas (see Figure 1).

Patrons of the Wild West got a bargain for their money. Not only did they get to visit the Indian camp, horse stables, and other places of interest on the grounds, and see the show, they also got a chance to purchase food, drink, and souvenirs from vendors on the grounds.

Food concessions ranged from caramel apples to samples of camp cooking sold at Major Burke's log cabin. Popcorn seems to have been the biggest seller among the various offerings when the show was in Europe. Drinks, both alcoholic and nonalcoholic, could also be found on the grounds. In fact, for a time, Buffalo Bill's Wild West even carbonated its own soda pop.

But the big money items were the souvenirs. Everything from books and sheet music to statuettes and peace pipes were offered and purchased in great quantities. Not all of these items were actually manufactured for the management, but all were prominently marked with Buffalo Bill's name. The practice is reminiscent of the tourist stalls that spring up around World's Fair grounds today. Not all of the material is sanctioned by the fair committee, but each item is designed to remind the buyer of its origin.

It took a great deal of equipment to mount this operation. Buffalo Bill's Wild West's official route book for 1896 lists the total amount of canvas, stakes, and rope it took to build this camp from scratch each day.

Canvas		Stakes	
Big Top	7,000 yards	Big Top	344
(Grand Stand)		Toe Pins	225
Side Wall	5,000 yards	Bronco Tents	96
Horse Tents	4,000 yards	Baggage Stock	68
Dressing Room	1,500 yards	Dressing Room	68
Side Show	2,000 yards	Back Wall	65
Dining Tent	2,500 yards	Dining Tent	68

Marquee	500 yards	Marquee	25
Engine Tent	250 yards	Side Show	38
Total	22,750 yards	Side Show	
20 miles of rope		Banners	32
		Engine Tent	10
		Elec. Light	65
		Total	1,104[8]

Along with the tents, the ticket wagons, the scenery, and the grandstand, the company had to pack, move, unload, and rig a great deal of equipment. All the lighting instruments and the portable generators, the large property items including the Deadwood Stage and the covered wagons, and the guns and ammunition had to be placed in their proper positions and made ready for performance.

The guns and ammunition were kept in the ammunition wagon. The ordnance master who was in charge of this wagon had many duties. His primary responsibility was to keep the guns used by the performers clean and in good repair. (He did not handle the guns of any of the sharpshooters who traveled with the show.) He was also in charge of hand loading the blank cartridges used in the battle sequences. These shells were packed with a regular charge but a rosin-wad replaced the bullet.[9] The ordnance master also loaded the shot into the cartridges used by Cody in his sharpshooting act. Another of this man's duties was to make the glass balls needed for the shooting acts in each day's performance. These balls were made out of melted glass, sulphur, and resin. Because they were quite fragile and took up a good deal of room, a new supply had to be manufactured each day.[10]

Because the large property items were bulky and quite valuable, they had to be moved with considerable care. In addition to the stagecoach, there were covered wagons, the locomotive and cars from "The Great Train Hold-Up" (1907–1913), the settler's cabin (also used in "The Pony Express"), the water tank featured in "The Buffalo Hunt," and the orator's rostrum. When the events including artillery, Arab acrobats, and Far Eastern vistas were added, such equipment as tightropes, Gatling guns, and desert tents were added to the show. In addition to the Indian teepees that housed the Sioux in camp, extra teepees were needed for the events featuring specific Indian battles.

The most important large prop was the stagecoach. There are many tales about the origin of the Deadwood Coach. Wild West programs claim that Buffalo Bill obtained it from Colonel Voorhees, the manager of the Black Hills Stage Line, and that it was the very stage of legend that had survived Indian attacks and robbery attempts. George Lanthrop states that Cody purchased a stage in Cheyenne (probably from the Deadwood Line) and that "he [Lanthrop] drove the outfit out to Crow Creek Bridge and Buffalo Bill and another man stood back with their Winchesters and shot the holes in the stage."[11] A thorough examination of the Deadwood Stage at the Buffalo Bill Historical Center, Cody, Wyoming, in 1964, showed that the "Deadwood Coach" had definitely been manufactured in Concord, New Hampshire (called a "Concord") by the Abbot-Downing Company. The date of manufacture was never completely settled, but it was no earlier than 1840 and no later than 1863. But there is no certain way to determine what use was made of this stagecoach during its years on the frontier. It was used in every performance of Buffalo Bill's show from 1883 until 1913, however, and while it was valued at $25,000 in 1895, it was apparently "a sagging, patched, and shored up skeletal remains of its once glorious self" even that early in its show career.[12]

The prairie schooners or covered wagons in the show are not described anywhere in detail. Photographs reveal what appear to be ordinary wagons with canvas covers. These canvas covers were used for advertising in 1907, saying, "Take the Burlington Northern to the Big Horn Basin" (Stimson Photo no. 1841, Wyoming State Archives).

The problem of putting a train in the arena for "The Great Train Hold-Up" was neatly solved. The train engine was a scaled-down version of the real thing and was built large enough to disguise an automobile which supplied the power to move both the engine and scaled-down replicas of railroad cars that were attached to the engine.

Photographs are the only source of information about the settler's cabin. The 1907 photographs taken in Omaha, Nebraska, by Stimson show that this structure consisted of standard theatrical flats hinged together to form a small three-dimensional cabin. These flats were painted to resemble a log cabin on the outside, but when the door or window was open the flat frames were clearly visible.

The watering tank used by Buffalo Bill in his "Buffalo Hunt" is mentioned often in descriptions of the performances in Madison Square Garden where it was "sunk in the tan-bark in the middle of the arena to simulate a 'spring'."[13] Again there are no descriptions of this property as it was used in the touring show, but photos in the University of Oklahoma archives show a large tub in the middle of the arena surrounded by buffalo, so it must be assumed that it was used on tour at least occasionally.

The orator's rostrum seems to have varied in size, shape, and position over the years. Sometimes it was little more than a soap box off to one side of the arena; at other times it was an elaborate affair in the center of the arena that had to be reached by climbing a short ladder. It is not clear if this rostrum was moved from place to place between events to keep it from interfering with the performance, or if it was left in one place and the performers were expected to avoid it as best they could.

Other properties were added to the show depending on what events were being featured in any given season. These properties appear in various photographs and lists, but little is known about any of them. It should be noted that only a few of these props had to be preset before an act began. Most of them were vehicles that could be driven in to the arena as a part of the event. Even setting up the Indian teepees and the Arab camp in the desert were made a part of the overall spectacle of the performance. In this way the Wild West performance could continue virtually uninterrupted from opening to closing.

The most complicated equipment that had to be mounted at each new stand was the lighting. The Wild West carried with it the largest private electrical plant in existence at the time. The camp, the grandstand, and the arena were all lighted with general illumination, and three carbon arc searchlights were employed for special effects and spotlighting. The Electric Light Department employed eleven men. The electricity needed for this huge undertaking was produced by

two 300 horsepower Morin Climax vertical water tube boilers, carrying a working pressure of 135 pounds to a square inch. A Worthington duplex boiler feed pump is used, and there is a Korting universal injector for use in case of a pump becoming disabled. Two 250 horse-power cross compound non-condensing Ball engines are used, trans-mitting power through four 16–inch double leather belts to as many 80 KW Edison direct current generators operating at 125 volts.[14]

The lighting instruments in the arena were all of the carbon arc variety, and there were 24 of these lights on each side of the arena. Each light was rated at 4,000 candle power, but only half the instruments on each side of the arena could be turned on at any one time due to the capacity of the generators. There were two additional lights focused on the backdrop at the end of the arena. All these lights were mounted on poles just in front of the grandstand in groups of four. Each lamp had a special reflector designed by M. B. Bailey, the superintendent of the Electric Light Department. Designed to remove shadows of the carbon arc from the image cast into the arena, these reflectors were "somewhat flattened spheres" of copper lined with "small sections of corrugated glass mirror."[15]

The three searchlights used to augment these instruments were also carbon arc instruments. The smallest was an automatic feed projector with 8,000 candle power, while the other two projected 25,000 candle power each and were hand fed. They were "especially built for easy and rapid movement" and were mounted on a platform above the grandstand canvas at the end of the arena opposite the scenic backdrop.[16] The searchlights were used as most followspots are today—to pick the stars out of the company, to emphasize certain moments, and to brighten up important scenes. But their most important use at the Wild West was to follow the glass balls and clay pigeons for the sharp-shooters at the night performance. The gunmen had to be able to see their targets clearly, and even more important, the au-dience had to see those targets cleanly broken.

Also supplied by the huge generators was the power needed to light 77 2,000 candle power incandescent arcs on the grounds, 800 16 candle power incandescent lamps in the various tents, and 400 16 candle power incandescent lamps in the grandstand each night. The lights in the camp and grounds were turned on at 6:30, the lights in the grandstand at 7:30, and the show began between 8:00 and 8:15 every evening.[17]

The preparing of meals at the Wild West and the amount of food consumed at these meals fascinated reporters who visited the grounds. Time after time, lists of provisions were printed in the local papers. One such appeared in the *New York Recorder* on June 11, 1894, and lists the amount of food distributed from the storeroom in one week.

Beef 5,694 pounds; veal 1,259 pounds; mutton 750 pounds; pork 966 pounds; bacon 350 pounds; hams 410 pounds; chicken 820 pounds; bread 2,100 loaves; milk 3,260 quarts; ice 10 tons; potatoes 31 barrels; cabbage 7 barrels; spinach 9 barrels; onions 3 barrels; eggs 570 dozen; butter 298 pounds; fish 720 pounds; green peas 2 barrels; succotash 14 cases; sweet corn 12 cases; string beans 12 cases; buckwheat 150 pounds; rice 75 pounds; vinegar 6 gallons; catsup 15 gallons; Worcestershire sauce 15 gallons; mustard 6 gallons; powdered mustard 15 pounds; pepper sauce 3 dozen bottles; jelly and jam 220 pounds; condensed milk 5 cases; pepper 20 pounds; sugar 3 barrels; salad oil 5 gallons; crackers 10 boxes; oatmeal 60 pounds; lettuce 250 heads; radishes 250 bunches; young onions 250 bunches; watercress 2 barrels; sago 20 pounds; farina 15 pounds; tapioca 25 pounds; olives 4 gallons; horseradish 4 dozen bottles; asparagus 200 bunches; tea 25 pounds; coffee 225 pounds; salt 100 pounds; pickles barrel; piccalilli barrel; mackeral barrel; pig's feet 1 barrel; flour 4 barrels; cornmeal 200 pounds; syrup 10 gallons; and pies 500.[18]

In 1897 it cost Cody from $300 to $400 a day to keep all this food on his tables.

The men who cooked all this food had no mean task before them. Seven hundred people had to be fed three times a day, and they had to be fed on time if the regimen of set-up, parade, and performance was to be observed. Breakfast was served from 7:30 until 9, lunch from 12:30 until 1:30, and dinner from 6 until 7:30. These meals were prepared by seven cooks, two pastry chefs, and two butchers. The cooking was done either in the range wagon, which was 26 feet long and contained four cook stoves, or in caldrons of 80 to 110 gallons each, or on steam tables with steam provided by a large boiler.

The care and feeding of the stock was just as important as the care and feeding of the performers. The draft horses and general riding horses were stabled in one tent, the broncos in another, and the buffalo had a sturdy pen all to themselves. There generally were around 500 horses traveling with the show, and most of these were baggage stock. They were used to move the show once it was off the railroad cars. In the circus, elephants are used to do all the heaviest pulling and lifting, but in the Wild West, draft horses did this work. These horses were divided into eight-, six-, and four-horse teams as needed, and special teams called pull-up teams were used for loading and unloading the railroad cars.

The most valuable animals with the Wild West were the buckjumpers or bucking horses. No horse can be taught or forced to buck for long, and Cody never used bucking straps on his horses.[19] For this reason, horses that would buck and did so regularly and reliably were highly valued. Cody would pay $2,500 for just one tameable bucking horse. Next in value were the buffalo. The herds on the plains were nearly extinct by the time Cody began touring his show. In 1887 a Smithsonian survey listed the Wild West herd as the fourth largest in captivity, and in 1892 Salsbury valued each buffalo at $1,750. The saddle horses were valued at $15 each, although some of Cody's privately owned stock were obviously worth more than that.[20]

Many of these animals appeared with the show year after year and were supplied weekly with "ten tons of hay, five tons of straw, 350 bushels of oats, 200 bags of bran, 25 of corn and 2 bushels of rock salt."[21] The horses were well cared for by staff members permanently assigned to the horse tents.

MOVING THE SHOW

Scheduling and moving the Wild West about the country was a tremendously complicated task. Plans had to be made nearly a year ahead of time to assure that the show could be booked into favorite grounds in the big cities like Chicago, New York, and Cincinnati. Advertising strategies had to be decided months ahead of time to allow for the design and execution of new posters and programs. The general route of the show had to be considered carefully to link together the city dates already set and to take advantage of state fairs and crop harvests where money would flow more freely. Railroad cars had to be leased, performers hired, stock purchased, and equipment gathered. All of these things had to be brought to one central location and rehearsals held—not only of the performance, but of the tear-down and, set-up process for that season. Possible problems had to be solved before the show ever reached its first stand.

Scheduling was the most crucial part of the planning process. Buffalo Bill's Wild West was competing not only with other Wild Wests but with several large circuses. If conflicts in routing could be avoided they were, but sometimes it paid to switch the route so that the show could precede a rival group through an area. This tactic could put the rival show out of business either for the season or for good, but it could also put the Wild West out of business if the audience members chose to wait for the other show.

It was a good idea to avoid sections of the country that had been played the year before. If the performances were separated by a year or two, residents of small towns were more likely to attend every time the show came to town. Management tried to arrange for a show to arrive in town in the best weather and at the best possible time of year. It did no good to play the Pacific Northwest in the rainy season or Iowa when everyone was in the fields harvesting corn.

The broad plan for the route was established months ahead of time, but the individual stands in small towns were arranged on a shorter time scale. The exact location of a performance depended on securing a suitable lot and enough supplies in any given community. The task of locating these things was left to the crews in the advance car.

Known as "the advance," these men traveled in one-day stands as well. They had to be the exact same number of stands ahead of the show all season, or the complex pattern of advertising and supplies would become hopelessly snarled. The advance had

many jobs including finding and leasing the show grounds, securing any licenses needed, contracting for supplies for the personnel and the stock, arranging for newspaper advertising, and
posting the billboards.

The advance car was a wonderfully efficient, specially designed railroad car that could be added to any train going in the
right direction at the proper time. It contained everything the
advance men needed to complete their duties. According to an
article in the *Cardiff Mail*:

At one end is the office of the car manager; at the other a boiler is
convenient for the purpose of making paste, should the show at anytime
go to a small country place where billposters and paste are alike unknown. Between the office and the boiler in the car there are large
lockers where hundreds of different kinds of posters are systematically
arranged. Above these are tables where the slips giving the name of
the city and the date of the exposition's visit are attached. Above the
tables, again, are the sleeping bunks.[22]

Once the show grounds had been found and supplies arranged
for, the crew of this car had to get the posters up. These posters
were the main form of advertising used by the show and were
essential to obtaining a good turnout at the performance. The
average number of sheets posted for each one-day stand was
between 6,000 and 8,000, and they were all posted in one day.
These posters varied in size and quality depending on the size
and quality of the show posting them.

The posters came in definite sizes depending on how many
"sheets" were involved. A one-sheet was 28 inches by 42 inches.
With this as the basic unit, there were half-sheets, one-sheets, 2-,
3-, 6-, 9-, 12-, 16-, 20-, 24-, 28-, and 32-sheets that would satisfy
most needs. But Buffalo Bill occasionally commissioned a much
larger poster. One such poster was 108 sheets, or 9 feet high by
91 feet long. Another was 168 sheets, or 9 feet high and 143
feet long.[23]

It is agreed by those who have studied show-poster lithography
that the posters for Buffalo Bill's Wild West were among the
best. Printed by the Show Printer's Association of America, these
lithographs were often quite impressive. Such care was put into

their creation that most of these printers had one man assigned to do nothing but sketch the detail work on the horses that appeared on almost all circus and Wild West posters.

This form of advertising was quite cheap by today's standards. A 28–sheet billboard cost about $4.00 to print. Then anywhere from $3.50 to $13.50 a month was spent to rent space to hang the lithographs, bringing the total cost of a large colored billboard to a maximum of $17.00 a month.[24]

The men in the advance cars rarely, if ever, saw the Wild West in performance, but without their constant work the show could have never left winter quarters. The general manager traveled back and forth between the show and the advance, constantly updating and approving plans for the next section of the tour.

Moving the show from one of these stands to the next was a major enterprise. Basic procedures for efficient use of railroad equipment had been well established by the circuses in America; and Cody's staff had only to adapt them to their special needs. The Buffalo Bill show needed flat cars for the storage of large properties and wagons, stock cars for horses and buffalo (and eventually elephants), and coaches for the personnel. These were arranged into two sections.

The first section included everything that could be struck and moved after the evening performance began and everything that would be needed first thing on the new lot. This included the cook wagons, the grandstand seats, the dining, dressing, and stable tents, the grandstand canvas, the side show annex, and the ticket wagon.[25]

The second section included the saddle horses, the buffalo, the large properties, and the Electric Light Department, as well as most of the performers and the executive staff.[26] All of these items and people were needed right up to the end of the evening performance but were not needed in the next town until the parade.

On the show lot, the various departments loaded their equipment onto specially designed wagons. Each tent peg, performer's trunk, and kitchen pot had a specific spot on one of these wagons. The wagons also had a specific order in the lineup leaving the lot. Those containing the items needed first on the next lot had to be loaded on the first train car, and therefore had to be first in line, and so on. The wagons were hitched to the baggage horses and taken to the train according to this strict plan.

Meanwhile, the train was being prepared for the arrival of the wagons. The flat cars were connected to one another by iron plates laid across the gaps between cars, and a ramp was positioned between the end of the final flat car and the ground. Pull-up horses were put into their special harness and positioned to receive the wagons.

As each wagon reached the train, the baggage horses were unhitched (to return to the lot for another wagon) and the pull-up teams hitched in their place. These horses walked along beside the flat cars, pulling the wagon up the ramp and across the cars to its place. The train crew then put chock blocks in front of and behind the wheels and the process was repeated until all the wagons were loaded onto the train.

The horses and buffalo were loaded into stock cars sideways rather than lengthwise, and close enough together to help each other stay on their feet as the train swayed and jolted along. The performers and staff slept in Pullman coaches, where the job determined the sleeping arrangements. A performer slept in a room with only two berths, but workmen slept in cars specially outfitted with tiers of bunks three high. Many of these men slept on the flat cars by their own choice, because the coaches were so stuffy and cramped.[27]

When the show arrived at a new stand, the unloading procedure was the reverse of the loading procedure. Once on the lot, the involved process of setting up camp and preparing the grandstand was repeated. This kind of touring was physically taxing and very expensive, but Buffalo Bill's Wild West and Congress of Rough Riders of the World moved across the United States giving a parade and two performances, day after day, for nineteen years.

CHAPTER THREE

ON WITH THE SHOW

At the very outset it is truthfully claimed and should be intelligently understood that Buffalo Bill's Wild West and Congress of Rough Riders of the World is, in its way, an absolutely distinct and original innovation in popular instruction and entertainment; an exact, complete and entirely genuine historical and equestrian revelation, many of the participants in which played brave and famous warrior parts in the dread and dangerous scenes of savage warfare, hazardous exploration and pioneer advancement which are so vividly, powerfully and accurately reproduced as to actually partake more of reality than of imitation.[1]

Stagnation meant death to a show that drew its audience from the same small communities year after year. The program for Buffalo Bill's Wild West was changed and adjusted constantly to cater to current trends and interests. But at the same time, the managers could never risk a total change of events in one season. A delicate balance had to be maintained by keeping events that audience members loved and had come to expect and removing events that had become stale and overused to make room for new ones. These new events were tried out during early performances in one of the least important places in the program, and if they were well received, they might be moved into a more important position for the rest of the run. If they were not well received, they would be left in their original places and dropped at the end of the season.

A careful examination of programs for Buffalo Bill's Wild West reveals that 86 different events were performed at one time or another between 1883 and 1913. These events fall into six major categories: races, shooting acts, specialty acts, military exhibitions, riding and horse acts, and dramatic spectacles.

Throughout the 30 years that the show was performed, the different types of acts given the main focus varied. During the early years there were races and shooting acts in abundance. The emphasis slowly shifted to riding and horse acts when the Congress of Rough Riders of the World was added in 1893. As interest in these acts began to pale, emphasis was placed on military exhibitions, and finally the dramatic spectacles became the most numerous and important events in the Wild West. Regardless of the major emphasis of the show, during most years examples of events from each category appeared in the program, although the first military exhibition was not added until 1893.

Working to give the events continuity as a show were the orator, the cowboy band, and the Wild West clowns. Through their efforts, transitions were made from one category to the next with a minimum of disruption. The clowns are mentioned only occasionally in newspaper accounts and rosters. Apparently they provided entertainment prior to the "Grand Entry" and may have appeared at other times to fill awkward pauses and to help keep the cowboys safe from rampaging animals, just as they do in rodeo today. During the period prior to the first event, these clowns appeared in the stands as "Samanthy and Timothy Hayseed." These characters would heatedly argue over where their seats were, causing much embarrassment for whoever was sitting in those seats, and then they would move on in search of the "privy."[2] Another clown called "Hidalgo" is mentioned in an 1894 New York newspaper article: "Hidalgo had a little mule about as big as a good-sized dog, and to see him mounted on this little beast, wearing his enormous Mexican sombrero and a pair of gloriously long-haired chaps, is to see a funny picture."[3]

The show itself began at 8:00 P.M. (or 8:15 depending on the year) with the strains of "The Star Spangled Banner," which was played by Colonel William Sweeney and his thirty-six member Cowboy Band. This piece was always used as the "Overture" although it did not become the national anthem until 1931. In this way, Buffalo Bill's Wild West established a tradition that is still followed at almost all outdoor entertainment events. Following the tradition of circus bands everywhere, the Cowboy Band

provided accompaniment for the various acts and bridges between acts. These tunes were carefully chosen to build the excitement and aid the climaxes. During at least one season (1902),
the marches of John Phillip Sousa were used frequently. The
band was apparently very good and was well received everywhere
it played, although reporters did not approve of its rendition of
"God Save the Queen" during the first tour of Canada.[4] The
Wild West would have been less interesting and exciting without
the musical accompaniment provided by the band.

It is the cowboy band which supplies the obligatto to the bucking of
the broncos, the raids of the redskins, and the antics of the Arabs. As
a matter of fact this band is very much above the average and amid
less sensational surroundings would come in for appreciative applause.[5]

After the "Overture" the orator mounted his rostrum and
began his announcements. His voice is variously described in
newspaper accounts as "a foghorn" possessing "deep bell-like
tones" and as "singularly loud and resonant." He used this voice
to "announce the items of the entertainment, and make matters
clear to the spectators unprovided with printed programs. He
also introduces brief, amusing anecdotes of the various performers, and indicates the tribe to which each Indian chief belongs as he comes bounding in on horseback."[6] Without the
orator much of the performance would have become incom-
prehensible to those unfamiliar with Western practices and events.
This man also provided another useful service. He formed a
friendly link between the audience and the performers. He was
able to focus attention on the proper place, so that no one missed
anything important, and he could fill awkward pauses with funny
jokes or little stories. By doing these things, he was able to help
the audience relax and enjoy every aspect of the show. This idea
was copied by rodeo announcers early in the development of
the sport and is still practiced with great skill at modern rodeos.
    When the orator concluded his opening remarks, he ex-
changed a set of signals with Colonel Cody backstage. This was
accomplished by the orator's waving a red flag that alerted not
only Cody (who was watching for the signal through a hole in

the scenery), but also the followspot operators and the band. Then the curtain was opened and the "Grand Entry" began.

Every performer appeared mounted on a horse in this event. The order of appearance varied from season to season, but the basic procedure did not. First a group of horsemen was introduced: cowboys, Indians, Cossacks, Arabs, cowgirls. They galloped around the arena to take their place in a lineup. As they did so, their leader or chief was introduced, galloped in carrying the flag of the nation or group represented, and joined the group in line as the next group was introduced. This procedure was repeated until all the performers but one were lined up in front of the grandstand. Then the great Col. W. F. (Buffalo Bill) Cody was introduced. He galloped to the front of the arena, stopped his horse, and swept off his hat as both he and the horse bowed to the cheering crowd. He then uttered the phrase that became his trademark: "Ladies and gentlemen, allow me to present to you a Congress of Rough Riders of the World." Cody turned to his performers and yelled "Go!" At this point the ranks of horsemen began a complicated riding maneuver called "the maze" that eventually took them out of the arena and behind the scenery. Cody was always the last to leave the arena in this event.

The maze was never listed as a separate event. It was simply the grand finale to "The Grand Entry," but it was an amazing feat all the same.

Then in intricate and amazing evolutions the horsemen whirled and dashed back and forth, performing difficult maneuvers so rapidly that the eye could hardly follow. The cowgirls swept to the ground for their handkerchiefs while at full speed and regained their seats without apparent effort. The Indians with feathers streaming in the wind created by their own mad speed, threaded the pitching, twisting mass of horsemen with unerring eye, their shrill whoops pulsating weirdly through the crowded pavilions. Cossacks and Cingalese, Dahomeans, Mexicans, South American vaqueros and American cowboys—they swayed hither and thither on caracoling horses in a magnificent flash of vivid and contrasting color.[7]

The performance then proceeded from event to event until the "Final Salute" was reached. This salute repeated the "Grand Entry" and served as a curtain call for the performers. The maze was simplified to a figure-eight maneuver, and Cody was again the last to leave.

Because the program order between the "Grand Entry" and the "Final Salute" varied considerably from year to year, it is not practical to describe the events in the order in which they were produced. Instead, the events will be described as they fit into the six major categories: races, shooting acts, specialty acts, military exhibitions, riding and horse acts, and dramatic spectacles.

Ten different races were devised for the performances of the Wild West over the years. Only four of them became regular events. The most popular of these races was variously called "The Grand Quarter Mile Race," "The International Race," and "The Race of Races." This contest always featured a cowboy, a Mexican, and an Indian, and sometimes included an Arab and a Cossack. These men were mounted on horses supposedly ridden regularly by their cultural groups, that is, the Indian on a paint and the cowboy on a mustang. The performers were appropriately costumed and their riding gear also reflected their cultural group. The race itself was unremarkable; it was simply an all-out quarter mile horse race. There is no evidence to indicate that this or any other race was fixed, so that the same competitor always won. It is not even clear if the same riders and horses were used from performance to performance, or if these duties simply were assigned to the nearest performers wearing the correct gear.

The three other races that appeared regularly in the Wild West program were "The Bareback Pony Race" between Indian boys, "The Race between Western American Girls," and "The Hurdle Race." The first two are explained by their titles, but not so the hurdle race. This race was handled in one of two ways. Either it was run by horses who supposedly had never jumped before—causing great excitement and interest concerning how they were made to jump, or it was set up as another international race where the interest and excitement lay in which cultural group was best at riding jumping horses. One of the participants in this form of the race was a rider dressed in the top hat and tails of a gentleman rider. The other riders represented the various cultural groups performing with the show that season.

There were six other racing events that appeared in Buffalo

Bill's Wild West. These were mostly specialty events with some unique twists that made them more interesting. For instance, there was a 100–yard race between two Indians. But one of those Indians was mounted bareback on a pony and the other had to run the race on his own two feet. There was a post at the 50 yard mark that had to be rounded. This gave the Indian on foot a definite advantage because the rider had to slow down considerably to make the turn and could never use the horse's superior speed to advantage because of the short distances involved.

Two races were run for their comic effect. In one, billed as a "Half Mile Race between Indian Ponies and Mexican Thoroughbreds," Mexican thoroughbreds were actually jackasses that the orator claimed cost "four shillings a dozen." The other race eliminated the Indian ponies and featured only the mules.

An event called a "Gymkana Race" was featured in 1899. No descriptions have survived, but the modern rodeo event called by this name is run on a course similar to a slalom course for skiing. The object is to be the first rider to guide a horse through the poles without knocking any down.

Another specialty race of this kind was "The Relay Race." The programs show only that four teams were involved: Filipino Woman versus Indian Squaw, Mexican versus Filipino, Arab Woman versus American Girl, and Cowboy versus Cossack. There is no indication of what distance was run or of how exchanges were made.

The sharpshooting acts were quite different from the races. The focus shifted from the nationality of the rider and the spirit of the horse to the skill of the performer. Eight different people performed shooting acts in Buffalo Bill's Wild West. The first was W. F. Carver, who performed during the very first season of the show. "Doc" Carver billed himself as "the champion rifle shot of the world" and performed an extensive exhibition of rifle and shotgun shooting. During that same year, Captain A. H. Bogardus and his four sons performed a sharpshooting act with the show. Little is known about the tricks they performed, but Bogardus did return to the show as a partner for the 1884 season.[8] Also with the show in 1883, Seth Clover used marbles as targets.

For the four seasons of 1885 to 1888 a young California girl named Lillian Smith was a sharpshooter with Cody's show. Only fifteen years old when she first joined the show, she traveled to England in 1887 and made quite an impression on audiences there. "Lillian could hit a plate thirty times in fifteen seconds, break ten balls hung from strings and swinging around a pole, and fire four times after a glass ball had been thrown into the air, breaking it with the last shot."[9]

The three most famous and well-remembered marksmen with the Wild West were Annie Oakley, Johnny Baker, and Cody himself. Each of these performers had a separate place on the program to demonstrate his or her skills. It has been said that Annie Oakley always appeared right after the "Grand Entry" to accustom the audience and the horses alike to the sound of gunfire. In fact, she only performed in this position for eight seasons of the seventeen she was with the show. Until 1893 she was usually preceded by Johnny Baker, a race, and "The Pony Express." For the seasons that Lillian Smith was with the show, Johnny Baker performed in the number three position, Annie Oakley was number five, and Lillian Smith was number seven. When Lillian left the show and Annie moved to the number two slot, Johnny Baker's act was moved to the middle of the program, where he never appeared earlier than seventh or later than fourteenth. Until 1888 Cody appeared fairly early in the program, but in that season his shooting act became a part of the build to the grand finale and was linked to "The Buffalo Hunt" and the final spectacle. This practice continued until 1904 when his act was again moved to a more central position and linked with "The Battle of Summit Springs."

Johnny Baker learned his shooting skills from Buffalo Bill and Annie Oakley. When he first began working for the Wild West, he was only fourteen and was billed as the "Cowboy Kid." He slowly developed an act that centered around trapshooting. Baker shot from many unorthodox positions, the most unusual being standing on his head. An assistant held Baker's feet to free his hands to hold the gun. A standard part of his act included finding a rock right where he put his head. He would get up indignantly, remove the rock, and reassume the shooting position—much to the amusement of the crowd. Somewhere in the program, either during Baker's act or Annie Oakley's, a contest of skill was staged between the two of them. The rivalry became well known, with the young girls rooting for Baker, and the young men for Annie Oakley. Annie always won; whether by design or skill will never be known.[10]

The best remembered sharpshooter ever to perform with Buffalo Bill's Wild West was Annie Oakley. For seventeen years she appeared in the arena and thrilled audiences with her incredible act. She always performed in outfits of her own making and she never wore pants. Her husband Frank Butler, an accomplished marksman himself, was her assistant, and their poodle George always did his part.

There is no complete listing of the feats Annie Oakley accomplished, but some of her tricks are well documented. She shot an apple off the poodle's head while he patiently sat up for her. She shot the ash off a cigarette held in her husband's teeth, and a dime held between his fingers. Annie Oakley also shot holes in playing cards and sliced them in half. She had six glass balls thrown up at once and, using three different shotguns, broke all six before they hit the ground. Another feat involved jumping over a table before shooting two glass balls that were thrown in the air while she was still on the other side. When bicycles became popular, Annie bought one and incorporated it into her act. She shot glass balls thrown by an assistant while peddling around the often uneven arena; she rarely missed a target, whatever the obstacles she had to overcome. Annie had a good understanding of showmanship as well. She always missed the same number of shots to help build suspense. She had learned from circus performers that the audience is always more impressed with the difficulty of the trick if the performer fails to complete it on the first try.[11] Annie Oakley loved to shoot, and audiences loved to watch her shoot. However, a near fatal injury received in a Wild West train wreck ended her show career in 1901.

Buffalo Bill did all his shooting from horseback. He galloped around the arena on a white horse, beside an assistant who threw glass balls into the air. These assistants changed over the years. Sometimes a small girl rode beside him, sometimes an Indian, sometimes a Mexican. But Cody had a very good record of hits, no matter who threw the balls or the condition of the arena. Captain Frank Winch says Cody shot better than 97 percent of the balls thrown for him in thirty years.[12] Apparently Cody never had a sight on the rifle he used in the arena; he simply pointed the gun at the target and fired, practicing a technique called snap shooting.

Much has been written about the authenticity of these marksmen. Because smooth bore rifles and fine shot were used instead of bullets, many claim these acts were fakes. But these same detractors have not considered the safety requirements of a show like the Wild West. If a sharpshooter is going to perform in an arena with audience seated on three sides, and performers and stock behind a canvas curtain on the fourth side, he had better be certain the ammunition he is using will not harm anyone. While a bullet might kill a person or an animal, fine buckshot with a light charge will only fall harmlessly around them. Cody particularly needed to use shot in his act as he had no guarantee of where he would have to aim to break the glass balls being thrown for him. Annie Oakley used shot for certain parts of her act, but always informed the audience she was doing so.[13] An expert consulted by Don Russell says Cody used

the .44/40 W. C. F. shot cartridges with a thin paper bullet which dropped off from the shot charge after it left the muzzle, but did protect it from leading the rifling. The charge was about 20 grains of black powder, a half charge or "midrange load" and ounce No. 7 chilled shot. At twenty yards . . . the pattern was about two or three inches across.[14]

The accomplishments of these sharpshooters may seem less impressive when it is clear that shot was substituted for bullets, but not many people could perform these tricks even with the slight advantage gained by shooting with shot.

Specialty acts were sprinkled through each year's program to give variety and interest to the Wild West. These events featured individuals or groups with unique talents such as throwing the lasso, jumping over horses, or building a human pyramid. These acts involved highly unusual activities that would not be seen elsewhere.

The first of these events attempted was "Roping and Riding Wild Bison" in 1883. Somewhat like the Brahma Bull riding contests of the modern rodeo, the event was well received by the public. But there was one big buffalo bull that no one wanted to ride. After trying unsuccessfully to convince the wary cowboys to attempt it, Cody finally decided to try riding the buffalo himself. He was bucked off and spent two weeks in the hospital for his efforts. The event was not revived in 1884.

Another exciting riding event seen during the seasons of 1883 and 1884 was an "Indian from Africa" who saddled and rode an elk as it kicked and bucked its way all over the arena.[15] This was the only event featuring a black rider in Cody's show until he added a black cavalry unit in 1894.

For the first five seasons, the cowboys also roped and rode "Wild Texas Steers" as a part of the show. One of these cowboys had another unique skill he demonstrated. He jumped over horses as they ran by him. He jumped them in ones and twos, and he jumped them in groups. This event was developed from similar circus acts and made to fit in the Wild West by dressing the performer in Western gear and calling him "Mustang Jack."

The best-known specialty act was "The Pony Express." A rider galloped around the arena carrying a pouch marked U.S. Mail, changed horses at one end of the arena, galloped around again and made his exit. This event was occasionally "dressed up" by adding a cabin to represent the posting station and extra characters to hold the horses and cheer the rider on.

Acrobatic feats performed by a troupe of Arabs were also quite popular with audiences. This troupe built human pyramids, featured a whirling dervish and a tightrope walker, and demonstrated techniques of hand-to-hand combat. This event was coupled with another international event called "The Dance of Nations" in 1911. The dances were performed by men and women alike, and each group of foreign performers did some dance to represent their country.[16]

Audiences may have loved watching the cowboys and Indians play a form of soccer with a ball six feet in diameter, but the performers dreaded pulling the assignment of playing "Football on Horseback."

Five cowboys and five Indians played foot-ball on horseback, a game that was little short of murder. Those redskins were out to win, and with a couple tons of horse meat bringing that six-foot ball at top speed to try and put it past Cy Compton, our goalkeeper, we cowhands came to have a heap of respect for it. Robert Little Dog usually was goalkeeper on the Indian side and it was next to impossible to put the ball past his big mount. The crippling came when both teams were pushing and the ball caught a toe or a kneecap as it ground by.[17]

Cy Compton's horse enjoyed kicking the ball away from the goal—sometimes as far as 30 feet—but the saddle repair man did not enjoy patching the holes this left in the ball.

In 1913 a variation of "Football on Horseback" was introduced. Called "Auto Polo," the event involved two teams of players mounted on the running boards of cars. From the description in the program, Roltz C. King and his company staged an act that showed off all the possibilities of the motor car, including "motor races, flying machines, and dare-devil driving."[18]

Riding a bicycle through the air was the special skill demonstrated by George C. Davis, the "Cowboy Cyclist," during the 1903–04 seasons. He jumped his bicycle over a "chasm of 56 ft., covering a distance, in the plunge of 171 ft."[19] The program includes a warning that Davis would not attempt the jump in high winds or heavy rain.

In the Madison Square Garden performances of 1910 an act called "Frenzieo" featured a young man who dived "forty feet through space, landed on a soap-stoned slide, and, landing on his feet, ran, waving his hand to the audience."[20] The event was too difficult to be repeated in touring versions of the show.

Jumping seems to have been a popular choice of activity for performers in the Wild West. In 1911 Fred Garner was featured in a "High Jumping Contest" with a dog and a pair of horses as competition. Apparently Garner always won.[21]

After Cody joined his show with Pawnee Bill's, several specialty acts were added to the program. "Mexican Joe" did an exhibition of lasso tricks, Ray Thompson put his troupe of horses through a complicated act, and Rossi's musical elephants performed. Both the horse and the elephant acts drew their inspiration from the circus and had little to do with the Wild West theme of the overall performance.

Buffalo Bill began adding military acts to his program in 1893. The first of these acts was called "Military Evolutions." In 1897 both the "U.S. Artillery Drill" and the "Sixth U.S. Cavalry" were added to the program, and they remained as popular features until 1913. The "Artillery Drill" involved a lightning-quick drill of setting up, firing, and moving horse-drawn artillery pieces. More dangerous even than "Football on Horseback," this event caused at least two performers to lose their arms when these field pieces prematurely discharged.[22] The "Sixth U.S. Cavalry" gave "military exhibitions and exhibitions of athletic sports and horsemanship on Western range horses."[23]

The most interesting military exhibition was performed by the Aurora Zouaves (later replaced by the Devlin Zouaves). These groups executed close-order drills to exhibit the usefulness of a national militia. They performed in a double-time half-step with whistle signals giving their only orders. The finale of their act involved scaling a wall by forming a human pyramid to get the first soldiers over, followed by a complex maneuver that allowed the remaining soldiers to be brought over with their rifles and rifle slings.[24]

An unusual military event centered around what is now the U.S. Coast Guard, but was at the time the U.S. Treasury Department's Life-Saving Service. Called "The Life-Saving Drill," this event dramatized the rescue of the crew from a shipwrecked vessel. This act required two pieces of equipment: a pole with a crow's nest at the top to represent the mast of the ship, and the beach cart that contained the necessary equipment to complete the rescue. The pole was set up in the middle of the arena, the crew moved the cart in position, unloaded the gun that would shoot the hawser line to the ship, fired the line over the crow's nest, set up their pulley system, and hauled a basket out to the crow's nest. The victim stepped in, the basket returned to the "beach," and the equipment was struck when the rescue was complete. This drill was meant to emphasize the skill and efficiency of the men manning the stations; therefore, no scenery was used, and no attempt to simulate a storm was made.[25]

Various other events were featured over the years. In 1898 a "Color Guard of Cuban Veterans" rode with the show, and in 1913 the Boy Scouts performed a flag drill with the Wild West. An event called "A Military Musical Drill" was occasionally performed, but little is known about it. During the second European tour of 1903–04, military exercises were performed by "Veteran English Cavalrymen," which included "tent pegging, heads and posts, and lemon cutting."[26] By 1911 these events had been concentrated into "A Grand Military Tournament" (later "Military Tournament and Musical Ride") which featured representatives of various U.S. and foreign military units that had won fame on the battlefield. These performers were all legitimate army men who either were given special furlough to perform or were serving their reserve time by riding with the show.

Events involving riding and horses played an important role in the Wild West. Nearly everyone in the audience either owned horses or made frequent use of them for transportation, allowing them to appreciate fine animals and good horsemanship. The horse also was linked firmly in the minds of the audience with the winning of the West. Cavalry soldiers, hunters, bandits, and Indians were all known to have roamed the plains on their faithful steeds. A show that claimed to present the West as it was would not have survived long without horses. There were three types of riding events in Buffalo Bill's Wild West. One type of event featured the Rough Riders of the World; another, fancy riding and trick horses; and the third, Western activities.

Most of the riding acts were those performed by the Rough Riders. When this feature was first added, the Mexicans, the Russian Cossacks, and the South American Gauchos each had a separate act in the program. The Mexicans centered their act around the great Vincenti Oropeza, who performed feats with the lasso. For instance, he could lasso four horses running abreast with one loop. These riders also demonstrated how they used the particular gear of their country by doing various tricks on their horses.

The Cossacks began their exhibition by sweeping around the arena with drawn swords and singing a battle chant. They then dismounted and demonstrated a native dance on a wooden platform that was put in place by two cowboys. Their dancing apparently was quite different from Western expectations and one reporter described it as "skipping about in an idiotic manner."[27] Once back on their horses, the Cossacks picked objects off the ground while riding full tilt, and one rider even stood on his head in the saddle while the horse galloped around the arena.

Finally, they played a game of chase in which one rider wore a white handkerchief on his back and the others tried to remove it. During this game, the riders rode facing either the front or the back of the horse, depending on which was most convenient at the time. This activity concluded with a galloping charge across the arena.

The Gauchos gave demonstrations in the use of the lasso and the South American bola (a rope with a weight attached to each end, which was thrown to tangle the legs of horses and cows). Two poles were set upright in the arena, and the riders each threw his bola at one of them. Then each lassoed the second pole while riding past it. To conclude their act, they demonstrated the South American manner of subduing a bronco by lassoing it and then winding the lasso around the horse's leg and pulling him over onto his side. The bronco was then mounted by one of the Gauchos and ridden to a standstill.

As the years passed, various other groups of riders were added to the show. The cultures represented depended on what spectacle was being featured ("The Battle of San Juan Hill" demanded some real Rough Riders, for instance) and what war was being fought (Cuban veterans, troops from the Boxer Rebellion, or whatever) during that particular year. The Arabs and the Japanese each had a separate place on the program for a short period, but as military exhibitions became more important, the Rough Riders were concentrated into one event. For the seasons of 1895 and 1896 this act was titled "Ten Minutes with the Rough Riders of the World," and each group had a few minutes to perform. In 1897 the time was reduced to five minutes and finally in 1898 to three minutes. As the period of time for the performances was reduced, the level of activity in the arena escalated. Early on, each group got a few moments of solo performance, but by 1898 all the groups performed at once, and each group could only hope to win the attention of audience members sitting closest to it.

For the seasons of 1903–04 the Rough Riders were put into an event called "Exhibition of Seats in the Saddle" where each group would demonstrate their equipment and how it was used. This was accompanied by an event showing the differences between riding side saddle and astride called "Exhibition of Riding—American Frontier Girls."

The fancy riding events were done by groups of horses that were trained in the steps of the Spanish riding school (called High School Horses). In 1887 and 1888 Emma Hickok performed with such an act, and in the final years of the show, Ray Thompson and Rhoda Royal joined the show with their trained horses. The horses jumped to music, stood on their hind legs, and knelt down to bow when given almost unnoticeable signals by their riders.

Three events demonstrated Western horses or riding practices. The first was only featured for the season of 1896. Called "A Horse Fair," the draft horses with the show were exhibited in this act. They were simply led around the arena in pairs, allowing the public to see and appreciate a number of fine horses they would not otherwise have seen.

The "Virginia Reel on Horseback" was performed sometimes as a separate event and sometimes as part of "A Holiday at TE Ranch" or "An Emigrant Train Crossing the Prairie." Both cowboys and cowgirls rode in this event, putting their horses through the traditional steps of the reel, with the band providing an appropriate tune.

The most popular event showing cowboys and their horses was "Cowboy Fun." During this act the cowboys picked up objects off the ground at a gallop and did some trick riding to demonstrate their equality with the other Rough Riders. But the most exciting part of this event was the bronc riding.

When a bronco out on the ranges of the West, by bad handling becomes thoroughly vicious, has earned the name of the "Colorado Cloudburst," or the "Dakota-Demon," the "Montana Man-Killer," or some such reassuring title, and there is not a bronco buster on the range who will tackle him, and he is not worth two trade dollars to anyone, they ship him to a "Wild West" show.[28]

The chief of the cowboys assigned riders to each horse during the preceding act and briefed the cowboys on each horse's bad habits. When the act began, the horses were turned loose in the arena already saddled and bridled, but the cowboys had to lasso them, mount them, and ride them without the benefit of the time clock, bucking chute, and pick-up rider that aid the modern rodeo rider. But then, these riders did not have to follow the modern rules dictating a clean ride, either.

The horse was lassoed first, then two or three men would hold it as steady as possible by holding tightly to the lasso (called snubbing) while the rider mounted. If the horse was particularly mean, the snubbers might throw the horse on its side, and the rider would mount him while he was on the ground. When the rider gave the signal, the snubbers would turn the horse loose, and it was up to the rider to stay on him. There was no way to get off one of these horses except to ride him to a standstill or be bucked off. From the list of injuries received during this act in just one season, it can be assumed that many riders took the second way down.[29]

Buffalo Bill's Wild West featured many women bronc riders over the years. The first appeared in 1887,[30] and at least one appeared nearly every season after that. These women were well liked by the audiences and highly respected by the cowboys with the show. They were performing long before the first women rodeo riders, who appeared in the early 1900s, and there is no indication that Wild West cowgirls ever tied their stirrups together or rode different buckers than the men, as was often the case on the rodeo circuit.[31]

The most complicated and lengthy of the Wild West events were those that told a story of some type. These dramatic spectacles incorporated all the other types of events in reenactments of incidents as they might have happened on the Plains. Sixteen different spectacles were staged at different times between 1883 and 1913. Some of these spectacles depicted general or generic Western events, such as the train robbery or the buffalo hunt, while others depicted actual historic events such as Custer's Last Stand or the Battle of Summit Springs. In the later years of the show, these spectacles were updated to include current battles like San Juan Hill or Tien-Tsin, or to reflect a growing interest in distant places like the Far East.

The stories were told in broad pantomime, but there was a definite progression in most of them from a setting of the scene to the actual event to a definite conclusion. The reenactments of actual battles were the easiest to structure in this way, but only six of the dramatic spectacles were of this type.

Buffalo Bill's duel with Yellow Hand was the first such event to be attempted. The actual duel that this act was based on supposedly took place during a cavalry/Indian engagement at War Bonnet Creek. While it seems probable that Cody did kill a minor Indian chief named Yellow Hair in this battle (the name Yellow Hand resulted from a bad translation of the Indian's name by reporters), it is certain the duel did not take place as depicted in the Wild West. According to the Wild West version (also published in Cody's biography and in other sources), the Indian chieftain challenged Cody to a one-on-one duel to decide the battle between the Indians and the cavalry. Cody accepted, and after both men's horses had been shot out from under them, they proceeded to fight hand-to-hand with knives. Cody won the encounter by stabbing the Indian. In the printed versions this victory was followed by scalping the Indian, waving the scalp proudly in the air, and calling "The first scalp for Custer!" In the Wild West version, Cody got the same effect by holding up the Indian's war bonnet and shouting the same words. In actuality, Cody exchanged shots with Yellow Hair during the battle, both horses went down, Cody fired a second shot that killed the Indian, and Cody took the chieftain's scalp with his hunting knife.[32] This event only appeared for two seasons, and may have been removed because the image it created of Cody was too violent. It is one thing to watch a man shoot Indians with a rifle from a distance; it is another to watch him stab an Indian at close quarters and then remove his scalp.

By 1886 when the Wild West appeared in Madison Square Garden, "Custer's Last Fight" had been added to the program. This event appeared periodically over the years, sometimes called "The Battle of the Little Big Horn," sometimes "General Custer's Last Battle." During a few seasons the event began with soldiers breaking camp and moving off to find the Indians, but often this was omitted and the event began with the entrance of the Indians, who were moving their camp. They would settle on the arena as a good camping spot and begin setting up their teepees. Once this was complete, the Indians held a war dance. During the war dance a cavalry scout appeared and reconnoitered. After watching the dance for a time he rode off to inform Custer of the Indians' whereabouts. Moments later, the cavalry burst onto the scene, the battle was fought to the tune of Custer's marching song, "Gary Owen," and the Indians retreated, leaving the dead cavalry soldiers and their white horses in a tableau in the arena.[33] At some performances this tableau was followed by the arrival of Cody and his cowboy troupe, who mourned the dead while the orator intoned "Too late!"[34] At other times, Cody played Custer and this last scene did not take place.[35]

Not until 1907 did Cody add a different Indian battle to the program, "The Battle of Summit Springs," in which Cody had actually participated. The event began in the same way as "Custer's Last Fight" with the appearance of the Indians, the setting up of teepees, and the war dance. In this case, however, there was the added interest of white women prisoners being tortured by the squaws and in some versions even tied to the stake. The scout who appeared in this reenactment was, of course, Buffalo Bill, as that had been his role in the real battle. He observed the camp and took the news offstage to the cavalry, who then entered. There was a sharp battle that involved knocking down teepees, a good deal of gunfire, dead and dying soldiers and Indians, and finally victory by the cavalry. Cody conspicuously saved one of the white women from being tomahawked, although the other captive had already been killed (as happened in the actual battle). As the smoke cleared, the cavalry gathered up their dead and wounded and retired from the field. After a short pause, the remnant of the Indian band returned to mourn their dead and remove their camp from the arena.[36]

Don Russell states that "The Battle of Wounded Knee" was staged as a part of the 1913 season,[37] but there is no mention of such an event in the programs and couriers, and no reviews of this "battle" appear in any of the scrapbooks.

Two other battles were staged in the Wild West that had nothing to do with Western themes but were intensely interesting to audiences at the time. Beginning just after the Spanish-American War, Buffalo Bill's Wild West began reenacting "The Battle of San Juan Hill" complete with veterans of the actual event. Cody staged "The Allied Powers at the Battle of Tien-Tsin or The Capture of Pekin" for the season of 1902, not long after the end of the Boxer Rebellion in China. In these battles the Indians played the vanquished Spanish and the defeated Chinese.[38]

Staged in two scenes, "The Battle of San Juan Hill" featured sixteen of Roosevelt's original Rough Riders, eight Cubans, three Filipinos, and seven Hawaiians.[39] In the first scene, the audience watched the establishment of the army camp the night before the battle. Once sentries had been placed and blankets spread, the black troops led the other soldiers in singing "The Star Spangled Banner." After a pause signifying the passing of night, bugles were sounded, and the men marched toward the hill, singing "There'll Be a Hot Time in the Old Town Tonight." When the battleground was reached, the Gatling gun crew set up their gun and the battle was begun. Cody, with his usual attention to detail, hired Tom Isabel to fire the first shot in the mock battle, just as he had in the real battle. After an exchange of fire, the American troops rushed the blockhouse (probably the same cabin used for "The Attack on the Settler's Cabin" and "The Pony Express") that represented the top of the hill, and San Juan Hill was won.

"The Battle of Tien-Tsin" was loosely based on the rescue of diplomats that were taken prisoner by the Boxer rebels in Pekin (now Beijing) in 1900. The program admits the actual battle was much more spread out and somewhat less dramatic than the arena version. This arena version was staged in two scenes that were similar to the scenes in the San Juan Hill battle. The scenes are listed as follows in the 1901 program: "Scene 1—Assembly of the Powers. Cavalry Drill. Camp Episodes and the Advance. Scene 2—The Walls of Tien-Tsin." The program also carried a note that "The colors carried by each detachment denotes the army to which the detachment belongs."[40] The colors carried were those of the Ninth Regiment of United States Infantry, United States Marines, British Marines, Welsh Fusiliers, East Indian Sikhs, and German, Russian, French, and Japanese forces.[41] These troops may have had representatives who actually participated in the battle, but most of the cast came from the Wild West's already large company. They stormed a set of large gates that represented the moat and wall that surrounded the city. The Allied troops were victorious, of course, and the beleaguered envoys were rescued.

Cleverly staged as a contrast to the battles and military exhibitions, "The Far East or A Dream of the Orient" was much like a circus pageant. But the spectacle was given added interest by turning an exhibition of strange animals and exotic people into a story. The act began with the establishment of an Arab camp upon the desert, complete with camels, donkeys, and children. A courier arrived and in extensive pantomime told of the approach of a group of tourists. At this point, the sheik rode in on his Arabian charger and directed his subjects to capture the tourists and hold them for ransom. The tourists entered, were captured, and a courier was sent with the ransom note to the friends of the tourists. An entertainment was then ordered to pacify the captives, and performers began arriving. Many specialty acts were featured in this entertainment. A Hindu fakir floated a lady in mid-air and made her disappear. Japanese jugglers and Arabian acrobats demonstrated their skills, and Rossi's musical elephants played their various instruments. At the end of the entertainment, the ransom money arrived and the captives were freed.[42]

Eight of the dramatic spectacles involved Western scenes. Four of these eight events appeared almost every year for 30 years. These spectacles formed the core of the Wild West, and audiences eagerly awaited them year after year. They included "The Buffalo Hunt," "The Attack on the Deadwood Stage," "The Attack on the Settler's Cabin," and "The Attack on the Emigrant Train." The other four spectacles were added to the show for a few seasons to lend variety, then were dropped in favor of some more interesting and timely event. These included "Phases of Indian Life," "The Mighty Avalanche," "The Horse Thief," and "The Great Train Hold-Up."

"Phases of Indian Life" was staged as a separate event before the great Indian battle sequences were conceived. This event allowed for the demonstration of how an Indian camp was moved and set up. Then a war dance commenced, a rival tribe was attacked, and while the braves fought, the squaws and children struck and moved the camp. Once these actions were incorporated into the larger battle events, this spectacle was no longer staged as a separate act.

Staged in Madison Square Garden in 1908, "The Mighty Avalanche" was spectacular but not very practical for road touring. During this event a mining town was presented on a snowy day. The stagecoach arrived and departed up the hill. The snow fell more and more heavily, causing hunters and miners to become lost and confused. Finally, the stagecoach tried to return to the camp and overturned on the mountainside, causing an avalanche. The avalanche thundered down the mountain, destroying the mining camp and burying the people and animals under tons of snow.[43] No information remains about the mechanics of this event. It is not known what machines were used, what material was used to represent snow, or how the event was managed.

The season of 1902 was the only year that Buffalo Bill staged the hanging of a horse thief. The advertising spoke a great deal of "Justice Lynch" and the practice of law in the West. The horse thief was portrayed as a footsore army deserter who found a sleeping cowboy's camp and stole his horse. Pursuing soldiers soon rode into the same cowboy's camp and, after the theft of the horse was discovered, pursued the deserter with renewed fervor. After a brief chase, the villain was captured and hanged, and the wronged cowboy riddled his body with bullets. This act was not well received by the public who thought it too realistic and violent for the eyes of women and children.[44]

During the few years that Buffalo Bill managed his show without a partner, "The Great Train Hold-Up" was one of the major spectacles. Major Burke explained its function: " 'The Great Train Hold-Up' is intended to describe in a general way any of the scores of train robberies which have formed a part of the history of Western development."[45] The beginning of the event involved choosing members of the audience to ride as passengers in the train. After they were taken backstage to board their coaches, the action began. First, the bandits made their entrance and hid themselves. Then the train chugged into the arena. When the bandits swept down on the train, the engineer stopped the engine, and the passengers were forced off the train and relieved of their valuables. The bandits, at least sometimes led by a woman, would then attempt to open the safe, finally resorting to dyna-

mite. The explosion brought the redoubtable Cody and his cowboys to the rescue, a brief battle ensued, the bandits were defeated, and the train continued on its way.[46]

From 1884 until 1913, Col. Cody always hunted the buffalo
herd as a part of the show. Sometimes the Indians aided him,
sometimes the cowboys hunted with him, and sometimes he rode
by himself. Whenever possible, a water tank was included in this
act to simulate a spring. Cody appeared, dismounted, and gave
his horse a drink out of his Stetson. After having a drink himself,
the colonel withdrew a little way away from the spring to await
the arrival of the buffalo. These buffalo were chased out into
the arena, and milled about for a bit, then headed for the water
to have a good drink. Cody rode in among them firing blanks,
and the combination of powder burns, smoke, noise, and habit
made them run out of the arena pursued by Cody.[47]

The most popular and long-lasting events in the show were
all similar to one another and to the dramatic spectacles already
described. "The Attack on the Deadwood Stage" (or Deadwood
Coach or Deadwood Mail) followed the same pattern as "The
Great Train Hold-Up." Passengers were chosen from the audience, settled in the coach, and the stage departed for its destination. Part way around the arena Indians attacked, the cowboys
and Buffalo Bill rode to the rescue, and the passengers were
returned, safe and sound, to their seats.

This particular pattern was popular and useful. "The Attack
on the Settler's Cabin" was begun by setting the scene: a woman
hung up her wash, a boy chopped wood, a man returned home
with game for supper. Then the Indians attacked, the cowboys
rode to the rescue, and all returned to normal.[48]

While "The Attack on the Emigrant Train" also followed this
formula, several twists were thrown in to make it more interesting. Called variously "The Wagon Train," "Ranch Life in the
West," "A Holiday at TE Ranch," and "A Cowboy Outfit Crossing
the Plains," this event often included several specialty acts. The
wagon train entered, accompanied by outriders. Visiting children were often allowed to ride alongside the wagons or beside
the drivers.[49] The wagons stopped for the night and camp was
pitched. At this point "The Virginia Reel on Horseback" or var-
iations on "Cowboy's Fun" might be performed. Songs were

occasionally sung around the campfires as dinner was prepared. Once in a while the buffalo hunt was even added to this event. But eventually the Indians rode through the camp, taking captives and killing the cowboys. The captives were tied to the stake or made to run the gauntlet while the Indians held a scalp dance. Finally, the cowboys arrived and vanquished the Indians. During the 1892 season, one of the rescued women mounted behind Buffalo Bill and was carried out of the arena in triumph.[50]

There were several activities available to patrons of Buffalo Bill's Wild West before and after the performance. For many years people could attend the free street parade put on by the company before the afternoon performance. Here they could gaze on all the performers and most of the animals in full regalia. They could hear the band and even see Colonel Cody. These parades were meant to advertise the show and entice people to the show grounds. Once the motor car became a popular form of transportation and the show grew to huge proportions, the street parades became increasingly difficult to stage and eventually were discontinued.

Once at the show grounds, patrons were entertained in several ways, including simply wandering around the grounds and looking at the people, stock, and properties. Many people made this choice with the hope they might catch a glimpse of Buffalo Bill, Annie Oakley, or one of the other stars. An audience member could also attend the band concert that began a half hour before the show, or, for a slight extra charge, the side show, or could see the gyroscope. (No information remains about this attraction, but it had a tent all to itself.)

The side show for Buffalo Bill's Wild West had many acts taken straight from the circus. There was a snake charmer, a fire eater, a bearded lady, and a mind reader among others. But there also were a few special Wild West exhibits. The wife and newborn baby of Luther Standing Bear were shown in 1902,[51] and Johnny No Neck, an Indian child who survived the Battle of Wounded Knee, was shown for several seasons after that massacre. A white man, his Indian wife, and their children also were exhibited.

The wide variety of events and attractions at Buffalo Bill's Wild West drew large crowds for 30 years. The combination of events from popular outdoor sports such as rodeos and horse racing, with the familiar side show of the circus, and the more traditional storytelling aspect of the theater, provided something of interest for an audience made up of people with widely divergent tastes. Cody and his staff encouraged continued support from this varied audience by constantly adding new attractions and removing events that did not receive audience approval. Thousands of people returned to the Wild West grounds year after year, attesting to the success of this careful mixture of ingredients.

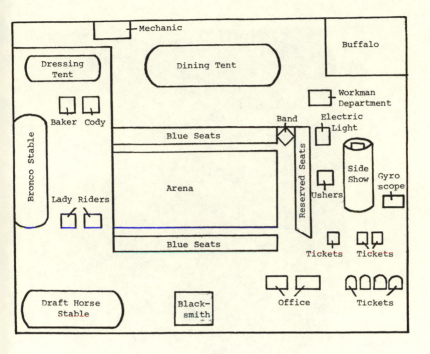

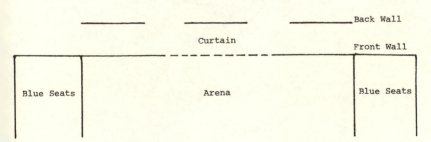

Figure 1. Diagram of the Wild West grounds.

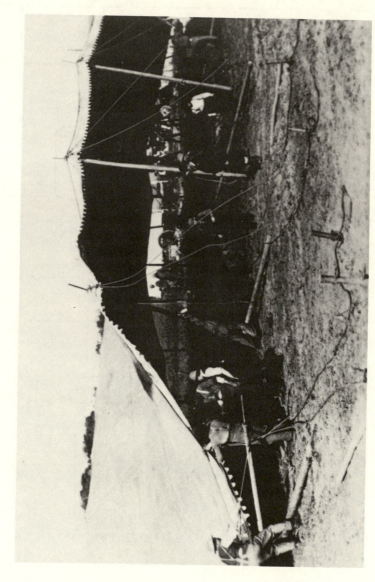

Figure 2. Setting up on the Wild West grounds; courtesy of the Buffalo Bill Historical Center, Cody, Wyoming.

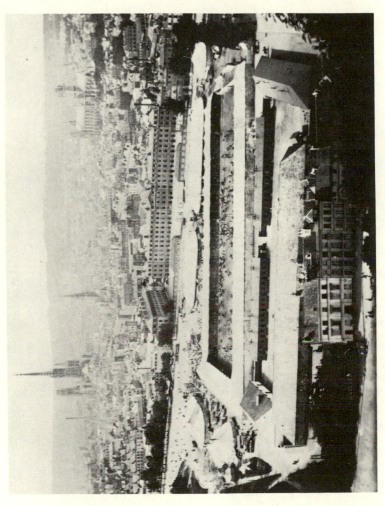

Figure 3. View of the Wild West grounds from the Eiffel tower, 1889; courtesy of the Buffalo Bill Historical Center, Cody, Wyoming.

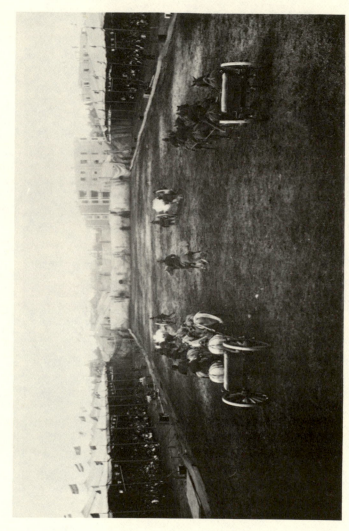

Figure 4. The artillery drill, Buffalo Bill's Wild West, 1907; courtesy of the Wyoming State Archives, Museums and Historical Department.

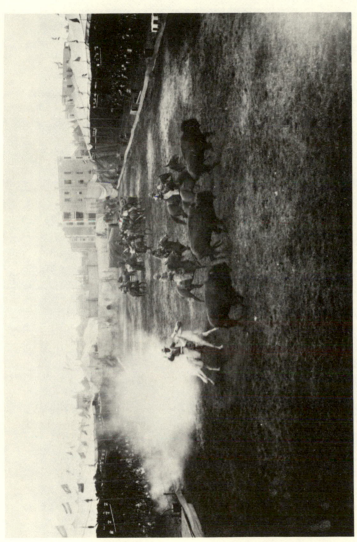

Figure 5. The buffalo hunt as a part of "A Day at TE Ranch," Buffalo Bill's Wild West, 1907; courtesy of the Wyoming State Archives, Museums and Historical Department.

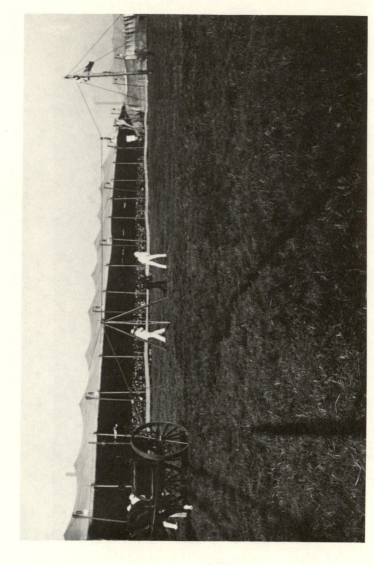

Figure 6. The life-saving drill, Buffalo Bill's Wild West, 1903; courtesy of the Buffalo Bill Historical Center, Cody, Wyoming.

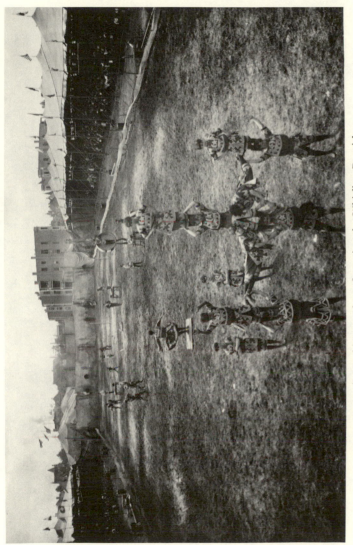

Figure 7. Arabian acrobats, featuring the Whirling Dervish, 1907; courtesy of the Wyoming State Archives, Museums and Historical Department.

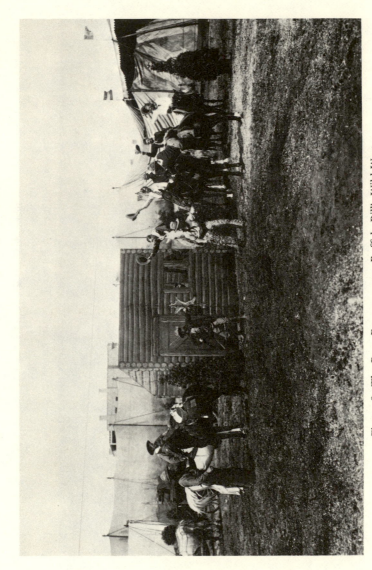

Figure 8. The Pony Express event, Buffalo Bill's Wild West, 1907; courtesy of the Wyoming State Archives, Museums and Historical Department.

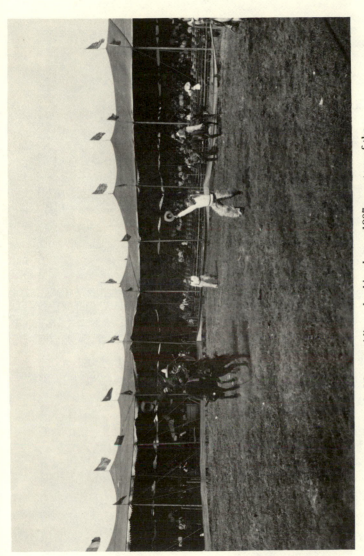

Figure 9. Woman riding a bucking horse, 1907; courtesy of the Wyoming State Archives, Museums and Historical Department.

Figure 10. The bicycle jumping event, 1903; courtesy of the Buffalo Bill Historical Center, Cody, Wyoming.

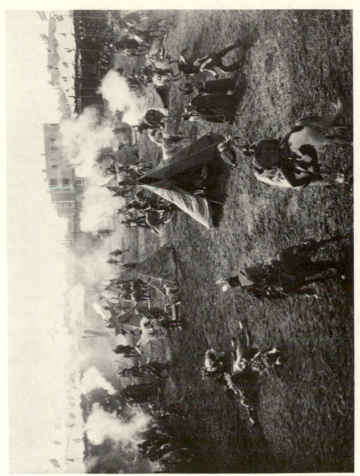

Figure 11. The Battle of Summit Springs, Buffalo Bill's Wild West, 1907; courtesy of the Wyoming State Archives, Museums and Historical Department.

CHAPTER FOUR

THE CONGRESS OF ROUGH RIDERS
OF THE WORLD

Col. Cody's exhibition is unique in many ways, and might justly
be termed a polyglot school, no less than twelve distinct languages
being spoken in the camp, viz.: Japanese, Russian, French, Arabic,
Greek, Hungarian, German, Italian, Spanish, Holland, Flemish,
Chinese, Sioux, and English. Being in such close contact every
day, we were bound to get some idea of each other's tongue, and
all acquire a fair idea of English.[1]

GENERAL INFORMATION

Cody's camp was not so cosmopolitan in the early years of the
Wild West, but this 1904 cast resulted from Buffalo Bill's de-
termination that as many things in his show as possible be completely genuine.

From the very beginning of the Wild West, Cody gathered
together as many frontiersmen as possible. He knew many men
himself who helped to settle the West, and these men knew
others. Once Cody began his search for company members in
1883, word spread quickly throughout the West, and men who
had been put out of work by the settling of the frontier began
to flock to North Platte, Nebraska. Old-time friends of Cody
such as Major Frank North and John Y. Nelson were given
prominent positions, and such noted Western figures as Con
Groner and David Payne were persuaded to appear in this new
entertainment enterprise.[2] Buffalo Bill made arrangements with
the government to exhibit Indians in his show, and cowboys from
nearby ranches eagerly applied for the $60 per month salary
being offered.

When the show was expanded to include the Congress of Rough Riders of the World in 1893, this passion for authenticity continued. Agents were dispatched to Russia and South America to hire actual riders from these exotic places, and later, riders were brought from as far away as Japan and Hawaii.

The same care for detail was expended on the military groups who appeared with the show. It was never good enough to have an unknown cavalry unit if members of a well-publicized battle regiment could be secured. Real soldiers, decorated if possible, always appeared, even if those soldiers had only been reserve troops.

But authenticity only went so far. The performers were carefully chosen for their reputations as fierce fighters and great horsemen. Thus, not all Indian tribes were represented but only the well-known Plains tribes; and not all Russians were exhibited but only the horse soldiers of the Steppes. Once the groups were selected and hired, they were dressed in costumes that were generally authentic but were often more colorful and showy than those worn for everyday work. The cowboys, for instance, always appeared in spotless chaps and sparkling spurs, and the Indians in the brightest war paint and the largest feathered headdresses.

When dramatizations of actual battles from contemporary wars were staged, as many actual participants as possible appeared, but extra troops and the enemy were supplied from the regular cast of the Wild West. Indians became the Chinese and cowboys became French, British, or American soldiers.

Only four complete rosters for Buffalo Bill's Wild West have survived. These appear in the route books of 1896, 1899, 1902, and 1911. In these years the cast numbered 241, 300, 266, and 241 respectively. In 1896, 1899, and 1911 there were nine different nations represented; in 1902 only eight distinct national groups appeared.

These performers all signed a contract with the show before reporting to early spring rehearsals. The contracts defined the job to be completed and the number of performances required each week, cleared the management of responsibility for injuries received in train wrecks and in performances, and stated that the first two weeks' pay would be retained by the management until the end of the season to ensure all performers had enough money to return home.[3]

The back of these contracts was printed with a list of rules and regulations that the performer was expected to follow. The performers were required to keep themselves and their gear and costumes clean and neat, and they were to conduct themselves in "an orderly, quiet, and gentlemanly manner." There was to be no fighting, drinking, gambling, or mashing (defined as winking, smiling at, or consorting with female audience members). No cast member was allowed to go to bed with boots on. These rules also stated the amount of baggage allowed each performer. No dogs (except those belonging to the Indians, who used them in the scenes depicting their villages, and for eating at special feasts), pets, shotguns, or chairs were carried, but each cast member was allowed one dressing trunk 18 inches by 18 inches by 24 inches and one personal trunk of the same size (but only if absolutely necessary). The performers were required to pay their train porter 25¢ a week for blacking boots and doing the laundry. Cast members were required to stay on the back lot during performances and were forbidden to stand about in the arena or grandstand. The final rule states that any person caught buying or selling any article of the Indians' costumes would be fined double the cost of the item. It would seem even the Wild West had its black market.

These performers came from all over the United States and the world. In the case of the foreign performers and the Indians, an agent was sent to find individuals who wanted to perform with the show. There is very little information about why these people left their homes, but at least one group of Cossacks toured because they earned more money than they could at home and because they were needed for only six months.[4] Some individuals and even some groups stayed with the Wild West for many seasons, and a few even gained top billing (Vincenti Oropeza—lasso expert; Alexander Kifouri—whirling dervish; Joe Esquivel—chief of the cowboys). Others fulfilled their contracts and returned to their homes or took up other jobs in the United States. (One example of this was George Hamid, a Lebanese acrobat with Cody's show, who later became an Atlantic City impresario.)[5]

The four rosters still extant reveal that the members of the Cowboy Band changed considerably over the fifteen years represented. Not a single member of the 1902 band remained with the show until 1911. Only its leader, William Sweeney, remained with Buffalo Bill from the band's first appearance in 1887 until the show was disbanded in 1913. (Bill Sweeney was an old friend of Cody's. They first met at Fort McPherson, and they both later settled in North Platte. When Cody decided to add a cowboy band to his show, Sweeney was a natural choice for the position of Band Master.)

In the early years of Wild Westing, Cody hired his cowboys from ranches around North Platte, but as the fame of the show grew and as rodeo became a more popular sport, the Wild West began to draw talent from all over the West. Buffalo Bill sometimes actively recruited famous rodeo riders, but usually these cowboys came to the Wild West looking for work. The job was more profitable and less strenuous than ranch work, and there always was the chance to gather together a stake to try the rodeo circuit.

The women with the show were of backgrounds as varied as the men's. Some came along to be with their husbands and ended up as the victims in "The Attack on the Settler's Cabin" or "The Attack on the Emigrant Train." (Or in the case of the Indian squaws, as performers in "The Battle of Summit Springs" or "Custer's Last Fight.") Others, like Annie Oakley, Emma Hickok, and Lillian Smith, came to the show as star performers in their own right. Still others came with their husbands as a part of a team. Among these were Georgia Duffy, rough rider from Wyoming, and Orilla Downing, who rode in the High School Horse act. A few others came to ride the broncs. These women were highly respected by other company members. Included in their number were Bertha Blancett, Lulu Parr, Goldie St. Clair, Mable Hackney, and Florence Shafer.

The many racial groups and the mixture of men and women in the Wild West camps caused many logistical problems. The married couples had to be housed together and given as much privacy as possible, the unmarried women had to be chaperoned and also given privacy, the various national groups preferred to be housed together, and some way had to be found for the groups to communicate with one another. Most of these problems were solved by the careful planning of the management and by rules that were strictly enforced.

The problem of language barriers was dealt with by interpreters. Each national group was provided with an interpreter who could speak both the native tongue of the group and English. In this way the management was certain that changes in schedules, routes, rules, or salaries could be communicated quickly to each group, and that each group had a spokesman if any problems arose. Because the foreign and Indian performers were totally reliant on their interpreter for information, these men became a mixture of tour guide and father figure for the groups. The interpreter had to enforce rules, keep his group together, see to their comfort and care, and generally assume responsibility for their behavior. Because of the grave responsibilities of these positions, the interpreters had to be chosen with great care. Their tact and leadership abilities were as important as their facility with the language.

The quotation that opens this chapter shows that the various groups did learn to communicate with one another, and research has revealed no evidence of serious racial tensions beyond the fact that blacks did not appear in the cast until 1894. In spite of the rule forbidding mashing, romances did flourish at the Wild West. Several marriages between cast members of different races and between cast members and audience members were held on the show grounds over the years.

SPECIFIC GROUPS

Russian Cossacks first joined Buffalo Bill's Wild West in London in 1892. The original group numbered ten and ranged in age from 18 to 25.[6] Their leader or commander was Prince Ivan Makharadze. They were contacted in Russia by Cody's agent C. M. Ercole, who made all the necessary arrangements for bringing them to London, and they were advertised as the first group of Cossacks ever to leave Russia.[7]

This advertising was disputed in several London newspapers. One man stated briefly, "They are not Cossacks at all, but one of the Caucasian tribes from the government of Kutais. Their proper designation is Kafkaskia Grousini—that is Georgians of the Caucasus."[8] Alex Kinloch wrote a long editorial that described his life among the Cossacks and utterly refuted any claim by the Wild West that its performers were genuine Cossacks. He ends his piece, "On being questioned by me, the men at the show confessed that they were not Cozacks [sic], and said they were Lisgins (a tribe in the Caucasus), and that they were not, and never had been, in any military service. Their peculiar accent and unmistakeable gestures, as well as certain movements in their dance, created a strong suspicion in me that they are Caucasian Jews."[9] There is no evidence that audiences were disconcerted by these counterclaims. It is probable that audience members were satisfied that the performers were Russian and that they could present a colorful and exciting act as part of the show. (The act was even more exciting than intended for the first few performances because Russian horses had not been provided, and the Wild West horses took a while to become accustomed to such strange riding habits as a Cossack riding backwards or standing on his head in the saddle.)

For the 1892 season at least, a man named Thomas Oliver translated for the Cossacks. He was born in Manchester to parents who were circus performers. When he was five, the family joined a circus that was to tour Russia, and Thomas was left behind in Tiflis. He spent eighteen years traveling about Russia with various performing groups and returned to London for the first time with Cody's Cossacks.[10]

In 1911 Buffalo Bill added a new twist to the Cossack act. He hired a sixteen-year-old girl named Arlene Palmer to ride with the Russians. She did all the same tricks as the Cossacks, the only novelty being her size and sex.

South American Gauchos were added to the Wild West in 1892. These riders were recruited in Argentina and joined Cody in London. Their horses were shipped with them, whether at the riders' request or because new stock was needed is not known. This proved a wise practice, and all foreign performers were provided with native stock thereafter.

By 1894 Vincenti Oropeza and his group of Mexicans were riding with the Wild West. Oropeza was the champion fancy roper of Mexico when recruited by Cody, and he taught many of his tricks to American cowboys. (Will Rogers was his most famous pupil.) Along with three or four other Mexican performers, Oropeza was in the Grand Fiscal of Mexico (a group somewhat like the Texas Rangers). Another member of this group, Severian Gonzales, had formerly been the horse trainer for the Mexican minister of war.[11]

The military groups with the Wild West were recruited from reserve troops and retired soldiers who had seen action in the uniforms of their countries. Besides United States artillery and cavalry units, members of the British, French, and German cavalry regularly appeared. Soldiers like Paul Winert (Congressional Medal of Honor—Wounded Knee) and Tom Isabel (fired the first shot on San Juan Hill) were recruited and introduced separately to audiences. They were made much of in advertising and newspaper stories, as well.

Cody often hired old friends and retired frontiersmen to appear with his show. Four retired Pony Express riders worked for Cody. Charlie Duprez rode in the Pony Express act in 1887, and Pony Bob Haslam acted as his advance agent in 1884. Marve Beardsley and Broncho Charlie Miller both rode as cowboys in 1887.

Tom Duffy and John Hancock served as stage drivers first in the West and then in the show. During the years that "The Great Train Robbery" was staged, the Wild West "secured the services of men who have at different times participated in one or more of the train robberies which have become notable for their daring and the consequences that attended them."[12]

Among these old frontiersmen was John Y. Nelson, who had been a trapper and guide, and was known among the Indians as Sha-Sha-Opogie. This man had tried his hand at nearly every Western occupation from scouting to buffalo hunting over the years.[13] When he joined the Wild West, he brought his Indian wife and children with him. Broncho Charlie claims Nelson was at least 60 in 1887, and he stayed with the show at least through the 1892 season. He rode shotgun on the stage and portrayed the besieged settler in "The Attack on the Settler's Cabin."

The show was protected from pickpockets and grifters by retired Pinkerton detectives who worked the crowds around the ticket windows and in the grandstands. From 1897 through 1899 this man was Detective John W. Rogers.

Women played an important part in the Wild West. They were included in most aspects of the show from running the conces-

sion stands, to clowning, to bronc riding. Women are conspicuously absent from programs and rosters as managers, roustabouts, or kitchen staff.

Most of these women performers appeared in more than one
act. "Ma" Whitaker, for instance, appeared as a woman settler
in both "The Attack on the Settler's Cabin" and "The Attack on
the Emigrant Train." She also served as a chaperone for the
unmarried women, a sort of camp doctor (dispensing home rem-
edies and bandages), and as a seamstress for the wardrobe department. "Ma" was born in Philadelphia and started her show
career when she married "Pa" Whitaker, who was a manager
for Barnum. The couple joined Buffalo Bill's show, and when
her husband died, "Ma" stayed on with the show.

The various cowgirls or "Western girls" as Cody billed them
rode in the dramatic spectacles as needed, and also did trick
riding, participated in "The Virginia Reel on Horseback," rode
bucking and High School horses, and rode in whatever races
were scheduled for them that season.

Buffalo Bill seemed to enjoy presenting young girls as a part
of his company. Besides Lillian Smith age fifteen and Arlene
Palmer sixteen he allowed both Eva Mudge eleven and Rose
Izett nine to perform in the Wild West. Eva was provided with
a soldier suit and a black pony named "Blackhawk" and appeared
as a performer in "The Attack on the Emigrant Train."[14] Rose
Izett served occasionally as Cody's assistant in his shooting act.
She rode beside him and threw glass balls in the air.[15]

Some women joined the show because they had married one
of the performers during the season. In 1892 one Englishwoman
married the chief Indian interpreter, who was a half-breed. A
newspaper commented in this way: "It seemed strange to think
of this fair-faced, blue-eyed English girl married to a man who,
although educated and in every way 'civilized,' is so closely allied
to the 'Red-skins.' "[16]

Once in a while a woman who joined the show would change
her mind. This was the case for Mrs. Thompson who had been
hired as an assistant in the wardrobe department. As the ship
was about to sail for France in 1889 she "fled down the gangplank
and refused to go on board again, saying she was afraid to take
the trip."[17]

Women seem to have been treated equally in the show and in the advertising. When they rated top billing, they received it, and when they could do a job, they were assigned it. They performed nearly the same feats of horsemanship and shooting as the male members of the show and filled in other necessary roles, as did their male counterparts.

Each year Buffalo Bill would hire more cowboys (particularly bronc busters) than he needed. Some of these men would never report to preseason rehearsals, others would change their minds once they arrived at winter quarters, and others would simply not be good enough to qualify as Wild West performers. The final number who toured with the show ranged from twelve to twenty-two.[18]

A few of these cowboys were Eastern men who had seen the Wild West and decided to learn the skills and join the show, but most of them were Western ranch hands who worked the Wild West for the generous salary. Many of these cowboys came from ranches near Cody's homes in North Platte, Nebraska, and Cody, Wyoming, because the show was well-known in those areas and the cowboys were aware of the jobs available to them.

The cowboys did many things after their first stint in the Wild West. Some married and settled in the East, some returned west to the ranches they had come from, some stayed with the show year after year, and a few like Buck Taylor and Si Compton (both chief of the cowboys at various times) started their own Wild West companies.

The Indians in the show received more publicity and attention than any other group. Both the Cody and Salsbury scrapbooks include hundreds of newspaper articles about the behavior, dress, family life, and history of the Indians with the Wild West. Cartoons, poems, drawings, and pictures of Indians were published in daily papers and weekly magazines. Indians in full regalia were taken to plays, banquets, and tourist attractions to make them highly visible and well-known.

Cody and Salsbury wanted Indians in their show for various reasons. Most of the events being presented required Indian characters (Indians were, after all, a vital part of frontier life). The Indians could have been played by white men (a solution adopted by Hollywood), and much trouble and expense could have been avoided. However, the Indians were one of the main attractions in the show. Nothing promised quite the thrill of seeing the "Indian who killed Custer." Without the Indians, the Wild West would not have been as successful. They attracted huge audiences of curious people and provided wonderful publicity material (both free press and planned campaigns).

All of this may not have been recognized during the first seasons, and real Indians probably were included as part of the push for authenticity. But it took almost no time at all for John Burke (Cody's press agent) to realize that any expense or trouble was worthwhile to keep Indians in the show.

There was also a concerted effort by the government to get troublemakers and Indian leaders off the reservations, where they were thought to be stirring up trouble and aggravating feelings of discontent among other Indians. The Wild West proved an easy solution to the need for an alternate environment for these Indians. Among others, there were about 30 Indians who were considered hostile, captured at Wounded Knee, who were forced by the army to tour with Buffalo Bill in lieu of prison sentences. He clothed and fed them and for the most part kept them under control, and the government had little or no additional responsibility.

It was hoped that these Indians would return to the reservations counseling peace and acceptance. But at least one Indian Agent, Daniel Dorchester, thought that the Indians were "rendered utterly unfit to again associate with the reservations" by their work in the Wild West show, adding that "the excited, spectacular life of the show, disinclines them to settle down to labor, and dooms them to the life of vagabonds."[19] Secretary of the Interior Noble agreed with Dorchester, saying "the Indian has greatly lost by such employment. He is taken into strange and most exciting surroundings; he is taught to renew the wildest and most savage scenes of Indian warfare and is too often to recur in practice to the lowest vices."[20] It is certain that the Indians saw much that impressed and confused them and they learned a great deal about the white man's world, but they were also encouraged to continue acting out their greatest victories and defeats in the arena. Whatever the Indians' reaction to the white man's world—awe, or disgust, or both—it is probable that they returned to their homes even less satisfied with the option of spending the rest of their lives on reservations.

Indians decided to join the Wild West for many reasons. There was little to hold anyone on the reservations, and the show offered money and excitement. The Indians saw the show as a way to keep from starving and as a way to keep their families clothed, fed, and warm.

Many Indians agreed to tour to learn more about the white man and perhaps help their people. This reaction varied from He Crow's saying he wanted "to see the lands where the palefaces originally came from"[21] to Black Elk's greater need: "Maybe if I could see the great world of the Wasichu, I could understand how to bring the sacred hoop together and make the tree bloom again at the center of it."[22]

The Bureau of Indian Affairs set up guidelines for using Indians for exhibition purposes in 1894. These required that a bond be posted for the safe return of the Indians (usually $10,000 for 100 Indians, although this price was applied to as few as 30 Indians), Indians be returned to their reservations by a set time, Indians be taken only from approved reservations, an approved interpreter be appointed to care for the Indians, a salary and traveling expenses be paid, food and clothing be provided, and medical attention be provided when needed. Also, managers were to "protect them from all immoral influences and surroundings."[23]

The pay was reasonable for the famous chiefs (up to $75 a month plus picture and autograph sales), but most of the others received less than the average national wage of $20 a week.[24] A common wage was $25 a month for each brave, squaw, or child.[25]

Travel, though paid for by Cody, was hard on the Indians. They were put in railroad cars that were stuffy and noisy and in the steerage of boats to cross the Atlantic. Black Elk was very frightened and distressed by his voyage to England with Buffalo Bill in 1887:

They put us all on a very big fire-boat, so big that when I first saw, I could hardly believe it; and when it sent forth a voice I was frightened. ... We were all in despair now and many were feeling so sick that they began to sing their death songs.

When evening came, a big wind was roaring and the water thundered. We had things that were meant to be hung up while we slept in them. This I learned afterward. We did not know what to do with these, so we spread them out on the floor and lay down on them. The floor tipped in every direction and this got worse and worse, so that we rolled from one side to the other and could not sleep.[26]

The misery of this experience was amplified by the fact that the Indians knew the legend that "if a Red Indian attempted to cross the ocean he would be stricken with an illness, his flesh would waste from day to day until even the skin dropped from the bones and the skeleton would never find burial."[27] Seasickness must have seemed to prove this legend to be true.

The accounts of Indian treatment are often misleading. They seemed to be allowed to go where they wished, but they spoke only their native languages and were unable to communicate without an interpreter. While Indian babies were often born on tour and were made much of by performers and staff alike, they were also exhibited in the side show to pay their way. Although Indians were given presents of horses and money at the end of the season, many died of diseases they were exposed to in foreign countries. Europe saw one side of Indian life, but they saw it through the conquerors' eyes. Some of what they saw was authentic, but audiences were not encouraged to see Indians as a people with an advanced civilization or as a group deserving treatment that was any different from what they were receiving.

The Indians continued to tour principally because they could make a better living performing in the Wild West than they could on the reservation. Young men were the individuals most often recruited, and the prospect of a life spent touring and play-acting was an exciting alternative to tilling barren land. Though few of the Indians toured more than one season, a handful of performers stayed with the Wild West from their first tour until their deaths. The rest toured a season or two and returned to the reservation tired, often sick, and bewildered by their experiences. Most of the Indians were overwhelmed by things they had seen that did not fit into their view of the world.

STAR PERFORMERS

Only three individuals were listed in the rosters as star performers. These were Johnny Baker, Annie Oakley, and Colonel W. F. Cody. Each of these exhibited skills as a sharpshooter.

Johnny Baker was a North Platte boy who greatly admired Cody and followed him everywhere he went when he was in town. Cody apparently took notice of the boy and gave him small jobs such as holding his horse and helping around the ranch.

When Buffalo Bill began assembling his company for the Wild West, Baker asked to be included. The boy was still quite young, fourteen, and Cody proposed to Johnny's family that he be allowed to adopt Johnny. Baker's parents absolutely refused but agreed to allow Johnny to travel with the show. Baker was with the Wild West during its first season, and as he grew up he took on more and more responsibility.

By 1902 he had been promoted to the position of arena director and was responsible for all final hiring and firing of performers, for rehearsing the show, and for handling all backstage arrangements during the show, as well as performing his own solo act. In this backstage capacity he was actually a stage manager on horseback. He cued performers, organized equipment and prop pieces, and kept the show moving.

After the Buffalo Bill show was auctioned off, Baker stayed with Cody, performing both with the Sells-Floto Circus and with the 101 Ranch Show. Even after Buffalo Bill's death, Baker remained faithful to his memory. He tried to put together a Wild West in Cody's name, and when this failed, he built a home and museum on Lookout Mountain next to Cody's grave and spent the rest of his life writing articles and giving speeches so that Buffalo Bill would not be forgotten.

The tradition of star women performers in the Wild Wests came directly from the best-known woman performer—Annie Oakley. Annie was an Ohio farm girl, born Phoebe Ann Moses, who learned to shoot to feed her family. As she grew up, she began to be pitted against the best male rifle shots in the area, and she slowly gained the reputation of being the best shot around. These local matches led to a competition with Frank

Butler who lost the match and married the winner. After they married, Frank and Annie toured around the country with several circuses and melodramas, selling their skills as a team of sharpshooters. In 1885 they showed their act to Buffalo Bill and were hired immediately. Frank gave up shooting at this point to become Annie's manager and ring assistant.

Except for the season of 1888 when she toured with Pawnee Bill (after an argument she had with Cody caused her to walk off his show), Annie Oakley performed as a part of the Buffalo Bill Wild West for seventeen years. She was only five feet, two inches tall and weighed about 100 pounds. She designed and sewed her own costumes, which were not always the height of Victorian fashion, but she never appeared in trousers or in skirts above her knee. This petite, carefully dressed little lady with a gun seemed interesting rather than threatening to audiences.

Cody and his publicity man John Burke made good use of this young woman's charm and grace, as well as her shooting ability. She was featured in hundreds of photos, programs, flyers, and posters of the show. She has been described as prim and seems to have been quite careful with her money. She never drank hard liquor but enjoyed an occasional beer. Annie spent her offstage time at such tasks as embroidery and gardening (during any long run, her quarters would be surrounded by growing flowers). She was very loyal to her husband and made their touring life as comfortable as possible.

Annie's career with Buffalo Bill ended on October 28, 1901, when she suffered serious internal injuries in a train wreck. After several operations and a year of rest, she had recovered sufficiently to appear in *The Western Girl*, a touring melodrama written by Langdon McCormick.[28]

Most of her later years were spent in Pinehurst, North Carolina, where she gave shooting lessons at a local resort hotel. During World War I she toured America giving exhibitions to benefit the Red Cross. In 1921 she was again seriously injured, this time in an automobile accident. Although she was told she never would walk again, she lived not only to walk but to shoot in exhibitions. Annie Oakley died in 1926, at the age of 66, and her husband, Frank Butler, died twenty days later. Her fame lives on in movies, comic books, and most notably in the Irving Berlin musical, *Annie Get Your Gun*.

The real star of Buffalo Bill's Wild West was, of course, Colonel William Frederick Cody. From his exciting early life in the West, he settled down to the life of a touring actor. In 1872 he began an eleven year career as a melodrama actor by playing himself in *The Scouts of the Prairie*. By 1873 he had formed the "Buffalo Bill Combination," his very own traveling theatrical troupe. Cody scouted for the U.S. Cavalry during the summer months and toured the East with a new play every fall and winter. Some of his plays were titled *Scouts of the Plains, The Red Right Hand; or Buffalo Bill's First Scalp for Custer* (based on the Yellow Hair fight at War Bonnet Creek), and *May Cody; or Lost and Won* (using one of Cody's sisters' name for the heroine). Until 1878 the "Indians" were played by people hired off the street. But in that year Cody began touring with reservation Indians. His final season as a melodrama actor was 1882; that summer he organized North Platte's "Old Glory Blowout," and the Wild West became his primary business venture.

It must be noted that during the 30 years that William Cody starred in his Wild West, he also was involved in many other business ventures. He established the town of Cody, Wyoming, in 1895–96 because he loved the Big Horn Basin and wished to see it developed. He felt that the newly founded Yellowstone Park should be accessible from the eastern side by railroad, and he believed that there was money to be made in such an enterprise. The railroad company would not build a spur until there was a town at the end of the line. Cody built the town (according to the railroad definition) by establishing a hotel (the Irma Hotel still stands), a newspaper, a livery stable, and a school.

Once the town was built, he founded the Shoshone Land and Irrigation Company to make the area more useful to ranchers and farmers alike. The project was not successful during his lifetime, but the Buffalo Bill Cody Dam above Cody now supplies water to the irrigation systems of the whole basin, making it a prime ranching country just as he envisioned it would be.

By 1902 Cody was busily working on a new project. He bought property in Arizona and formed the Cody-Dyer Mining and

Milling Company to mine for gold. Again the business was not successful during his lifetime, and the enterprise ate up most of Buffalo Bill's Wild West profits.

After his show was auctioned off in 1913, Cody went into the movie-making business. With the money of Harry Tammen of the *Denver Post* and the help of the Essanay Film Company of Chicago, the Colonel W. F. Cody (Buffalo Bill) Historical Pictures Company was founded. Eight one-reel subjects were made, mostly based on events in Cody's life, and they were shown with moderate success when completed.[29]

In addition to the ranch he already owned in North Platte, he also bought a ranch in Cody (called the TE) and a hunting lodge (called Pahaska Tepee) just outside Yellowstone Park. Paul Fees, curator of the Buffalo Bill Museum, observes: "He symbolized the past to millions of people but he really wasn't much interested in it himself. Basically he was a developer."[30]

But it was as a showman that Cody was best known. "From 1883 until the last season in 1916, Buffalo Bill was the star in his Wild West. It was to become the most sensational and widely seen show, witnessed by more than 50 million people in over 1,000 cities in about 12 countries."[31] In the first 26 years he missed only nine performances.[32]

Cody served in many capacities for the Wild West. Not only did he appear in many of the events in each day's program, but he rode in the preshow parade, talked and shook hands with as many audience members as possible, and appeared at parties and banquets in his honor everywhere he went. He allowed himself to be interviewed by reporters and photographed with children, and he answered the many personal letters he received. Programs, posters, flyers, and couriers all bore his likeness, and advertisements for everything from gunpowder to Parker Pens bore his endorsement. Besides being the show's main attraction, he attended to management duties as well.

Buffalo Bill Cody had great personal charm. Audiences came to the Wild West not only to see the exciting races and dramatic spectacles, but to see Buffalo Bill himself. Cody was a great horseman and apparently it was a joy to watch him ride. According to one contemporary,

He is the complete restoration of the Centaur. No one that I ever saw so adequately fulfills to the eye all the conditions of picturesque beauty, absolute grace and perfect identity with his animal.... Motion swings into music with him. He is the only man who rides as if he couldn't help it, and the sculptor and the soldier had jointly come together in his act.[33]

Film footage of Cody riding in the Wild West and the preshow parade supports this claim.

There are several allegations in the Wild West literature that Cody employed a double. Don Holm says that Dr. William DeVeny actually fulfilled some of Cody's Western engagements,[34] and an article in the Denver Public Library's Cody file says that Si Compton sometimes doubled for Cody during performances.[35] Research has revealed no pictures, program notes, contemporary articles or letters that support either of these claims.

Another story for which there is no substantiating evidence is that Cody resorted to wearing a wig when his hair began to thin. Although several authors have repeated this tale—including a description of the wig coming off during a performance—no newspaper seems to have reported the event (surely a notable one), and no photographs of Cody after 1900 conclusively show that he used a hairpiece, although this myth was recently perpetuated in Robert Altman's film *Buffalo Bill and the Indians, or Sitting Bull's History Lesson.*

Cody certainly knew the value of his personal appearance, however. In 1911 he brought suit in the Supreme Court of New York against the Yankee Film Company for presenting his image in one of their films. Claiming "the moustache and goatee and other distinguishing features of Buffalo Bill constitute a valuable trade asset and should not be used by others," the suit was upheld by the court, which stated that "Buffalo Bill has a sort of copyright on goatees of the peculiar form and color that adorn his chin."[36]

Whether his good looks were natural or aided by a wig, Buffalo Bill combined his reputation as a genuine frontiersman with his personal charm and his natural instinct for showmanship to make of himself a larger-than-life hero who was also quite accessible to the people. His personality provided the catalyst for a show composed of many disparate events and people. Through the Wild West, Cody was able to give the American people a taste of what it had been like to be on the Western frontier.

CHAPTER FIVE

PARTNERS AND FRIENDS

The crowd that attended the Wild West exhibition Friday has been variously estimated at from five to twenty-five thousand, but a crowd is one of the most treacherous things to estimate. Good judges, men who have experience in handling crowds, estimate the number to be somewhere between eight and twelve thousand persons. But whatever the crowd was, this much is true, that the management sent out $5,500 in silver via the United States express Friday evening, consigned to the Chatham National Bank in New York. The silver weighed 374 pounds, and the express charges were $22.[1]

Although it is known that Nate Salsbury insisted on double-entry account books for the Wild West, these books have disappeared. For this reason it is not possible to list accurate attendance figures or profit margins for any but a few seasons. General attendance figures were listed as a part of each route book, but only four of these survive, and the information includes only the number of performances and the total seating capacity of the grandstand in three of these. When the show was a new entertainment enterprise, overall attendance figures appeared often in the newspapers as a way of charting its success. In later years, occasional articles like the one quoted above appear in the scrapbooks, but few of them are as careful to qualify their estimates as this one. (For instance, press estimates of attendance on opening day at Staten Island in 1888 varied from 15,000 to 30,000.) Some information can be gathered from canceled checks contained in the collections of the Buffalo Bill Historical Center and the University of Oklahoma.[2] The only other information available comes from a between-seasons ledger showing cowboys' salaries and livery expenses, and personal letters from various Wild West personnel to their friends and families.

What emerges from a compilation of all of these scraps of information is a very sketchy outline of a show first struggling to establish itself (the Wild West was apparently $60,000 in debt by the end of the second season[3]), then becoming a very successful business enterprise (168,956 people saw the show during the first two weeks of the 1898 season[4]), and finally a company put on the auction block to raise the $60,000 needed to pay off creditors.

Canceled checks show that Cody was able to spend at least $13,133.90 between January 15 and April 5, 1894, out of his personal account in North Platte.[5] Most of this money was spent either on family members (Helen Cody Westmore received $2,000) or on various employees of the Wild West (Frank Hammitt $1,600, Lew Parker $500, John Burke $50, J. A. Goodman $700). Cody apparently wrote only one $25 check to himself during this period.

Other canceled checks and deposit receipts show that Gordon Lillie and his silent partner Thomas Smith received checks for at least $52,246.75 from the Wild West between January and May of 1910.[6] Between August and November 1910 the Wild West made deposits of $115,947.76 with the Fidelity Trust Company of New York.

This four-month figure was attained through the sale of 50¢ general admission seats, $1.00 reserved seats, and the various concession items made available on the grounds. When the show was presented in Madison Square Garden, additional profits were possible. Reserved seats were sold for 75¢, $1.00, or $1.50 according to location, and box seats went for $8, $10, or $12 on the first tier (also according to location) and $5 on the second tier. All these boxes could accommodate up to six persons.[7]

The Wild West was not only taking in money, however. Many expenses had to be covered before the management could claim its profits. In 1892 Nate Salsbury told a newspaper reporter what it would cost to start a Wild West of his own.

You would want $150,000 as a start, and as you are inexperienced in the business it would probably take you a year to get all your people

and animals together. We could do it in three weeks by cable. Here are
a few statistics. You would need 300 people—Indians, cowboys, Mexicans, etc. and be prepared to pay $9,000 a week in wages. As a matter
of fact we pay all our wages monthly. The Indian chief gets $100 a
month and all keep, the cowboys $80 to $120 a month and food, and
so on. You would have to bring them across the herring pond [Atlantic
Ocean]. The whole vessel would be wanted and your passage across
would cost $31,150.

You must advertise. We keep forty men out posting. In six months
we will have spent from $750,000 to $875,000 in advertising. The bills
on the London hoardings alone just now cost for printing alone $400,000,
and we have 80 tons of placards in the stores ready for immediate use.

Powder and shot? Yes; we make all the glass balls which are shot at
on the premises. From 42,000 to 45,000 are wanted every month. The
shot and powder bill amounts to over $500 a week. A first-class exhi-
bition "shot"—either man or woman—is worth $375 a week.

There's the cost of a thousand loads of cinder to put down on the
ground. You would have to buy 300 lbs. of paint to put on your big
canvas scene at the back, and by-the-bye, there is the canvas for over
40 tents in which your company sleep. Of course you would not want
to stay in the same place for good, so if you cared to make a railroad
journey to another spot with your show, just book 95 carriages and
wagons. Take your own portable grandstand—that costs $25,000.[8]

The one weekly statement of Buffalo Bill's Wild West and
Pawnee Bill's Far East that has been found shows that for the
week of June 1, 1913, the Wild West took in $22,962.09. But
for that same week they paid out $20,526.92. This left a profit
of only $2,435.17 for an entire week. This same weekly statement
shows that performers were paid a total of $3,593.15 and work-
men received $889.75 in salaries for that week.[9] Within six weeks
of this date the Wild West was attached by the United States
Printing and Lithography Company for nonpayment of printing
bills.

The head of each department kept careful records of what
was bought and sold, and what commodities were consumed.
These books were in turn audited on a regular basis by the
management of the show, so that they could know at a glance
"what it was costing them to give living pictures of Western and
international history."[10]

The publicity department kept records as well. In the 1907

program they were able to claim that Buffalo Bill had personally appeared in more cities, towns, and countries and had been seen by more people than any other man that ever lived. The program goes on to substantiate this claim by stating that from 5,000 to 10,000 people a day attended the exposition in Chicago—with as many as 52,000 being counted in one day; and as many as 65,000 attended one show in London.[11]

The top management of the Wild West changed several times over the years, and so did the general staff. Once again route books and a few programs give the only complete listings of the management personnel, and a few extra names can be gleaned from the autobiographies of such people as Dexter Fellows and Charles Griffin. For the most part, these sources list only the name and title of each employee, and it is not always clear exactly what tasks each job entailed. But from newspaper articles, autobiographies, and circus practice, it is possible to reconstruct the duties of most of these men.

The 1886 program lists only eight men as part of the management of the Wild West. There was a general manager, a business representative, a general agent, a treasurer, a contracting agent, an orator, and a director, as well as the two proprietors.[12] By 1911 this management group had grown to fifteen. Besides those positions already listed, an arenic director, assistant treasurer, auditor, master of privileges, historian, story man, and secretary/excursion agent had been added.[13]

During the years that James Bailey had a part in the management of the Wild West the number of general staff positions was greatly increased because each organization had to be represented in key positions. Route books show that during these years both Bailey and Cody had a business manager and a treasurer. During 1899 there were also a secretary and an accountant for each group, but this practice had been dropped by 1902, when Cody supplied the secretary and Bailey the accountant.

It was the general manager's duty to keep the Wild West running in camp. He had to be sure supplies that were ordered were delivered, rules that were issued were followed, and that preparations that were needed for each performance were completed. If the cook tent ran low on eggs, for instance, it was his job to supply more. If the publicity department made arrangements for some group to tour the grounds, it was the general manager's job to organize the tour, notify the company, arrange for extra meals to be served if necessary, and to conduct the tour itself.

Major John Burke held this position with Buffalo Bill's Wild West from 1883 until 1913. He is one of three people (Cody, Baker, and Burke) who stayed with the show for the entire thirty years of its existence. Burke first met Cody as the manager of Buffalo Bill's leading lady (Mlle. Morlacchi) in the melodrama *Scouts of the Prairie* and continued his association with the scout from that time onward.

Major Burke was born in Washington, D.C., and made his living as a stock actor (referred to as a "black-face Bowery song and dance man" by one source[14]), a newspaper editor, and as the manager of melodrama actors before he met Cody. Both the nickname "Arizona" and the title "Major" were purely complimentary and had nothing to do with his origins or his career.

Although Burke's position was general manager, his real use to the show was twofold: he wrote reams of copy (all extremely florid and containing many exaggerations and inconsistencies) for programs, flyers, newspapers, and magazines—all of it highly complimentary to Cody; and he developed friendships with hundreds of newspaper people all over the country, who helped to make Cody's name a household word. It is still possible to pick out those articles and parts of the program for which Burke was responsible by his unmistakable style. He exploited Cody's fame in every way possible and became a minor figure of note in his own right. While Salsbury disliked his exaggerations, Gordon Lillie respected his value to the show and acknowledged his right to be the "highest salaried Press Agent in show business."[15] He died in Washington, D.C., six weeks after Cody and was buried with honors by the Elks lodge of that city.

The position of business representative or business manager involved overseeing the expenditures of money. It was these men who set the budgets, decided which projects or departments were to receive additional funds, bargained with railroad companies and commodities suppliers for the cheapest prices, and generally kept the show on a solid business footing.

These men were aided by several other staff members. The

treasurer and his assistant kept track of daily receipts, the accountant and auditor were responsible for checking the books and keeping a running total of credits and debits, and the general agent, contracting agent, and railroad contractor helped locate and purchase supplies and transportation.

For many years Buffalo Bill's treasurer was Jules Keen. Another member of Cody's melodrama troupe, Keen had played the part of the comic Dutchman in *The Prairie Waif* during the winter of 1885–86. He is listed as a performer in the Wild West program of 1886, but thereafter served only as treasurer. Keen and Burke were not the only melodrama actors who ended up in management positions with Buffalo Bill's Wild West.

Frank Small, advance agent, is now press agent for Buffalo Bill, and Edward Q. Cordner, assistant to Major Burke, was with Henry Mapleson and other attractions. Albert Scheible, business manager, is a graduate of the Arch Street Theatre, Philadelphia, and was manager of Salsbury's "Troubadors." Fred Bryton, who has appeared in many companies as well, as a star, has the restaurant and refreshment privilege, and Fred Bowman, Lew Parker, Fred Ames, Matt Snyder, and others of the Wild West were formerly known in theatrical fields.[16]

The arenic director really served as a stage manager and director. He kept the backstage organized, rehearsed new acts, kept the show moving, and made final decisions about hiring and firing performers. Johnny Baker filled this position for Cody and shared his duties with the star, who liked to be a part of the performance management team. Another member of this team was the orator, who introduced acts, filled in spaces between acts with humorous patter, and signaled the backstage crew about what was happening in the arena. This team would not have been complete without the superintendent of the grounds. He was responsible for the condition of the arena (smoothing it when possible, keeping the dust down, warning the performers of obstacles), and keeping the grandstand clean and safe.

Besides these general staff members, there were department heads who helped to manage the show. The manager of the privileges was responsible for the affairs of the side show, concessions, and what was known as the "pie car." The pie car was a store where company members could buy candy, newspapers, soap, and other necessary items. He was supported in this job by the superintendent of the confectionery department, who looked after the affairs of the concessioners who sold candy items on the grounds.

The dining tent was seen to by the caterer and the head waiter, while the cook tent was run by the head cook. Once on the train, the comfort of the performers was superintended by the head porter and his staff. Costumes and properties were each seen to by an assigned department head, as was the ammunition.

In order to move the show and keep the equipment in top running condition, it was necessary to assign department heads to deal with problems and supplies in various areas. Besides the master of transportation, who was in charge of moving the show to and from the train, there was a master mechanic, a super-intendent of electric light, a superintendent of canvas, a super-intendent of baggage stock, and a superintendent of bronco stock.

The press department of the Wild West was quite large, since it included not only the press agent and his staff but the adver-tising cars. Traveling with the show were Major Burke (who was variously listed as historian, press writer, and press agent in the route books), a press agent who dealt with local newspapers once the show reached its destination, a general contracting agent who placed paid advertising in newspapers and magazines, and an excursion agent who arranged special rates for audience members on whatever public transportation existed between the town and the show grounds (ferries, streetcars, or whatever).

This staff had the collective responsibility of preparing pro-grams (often 60 pages or more in length and costing audience members a dime), heralds (a single sheet handbill), and couriers (advertising booklets). While much of the text in the couriers and programs was repeated from year to year, there were im-aginative touches added, such as cutting the pages in the shape of a buffalo or Indian head, or adding material about the newest event. These programs and couriers are fascinating to read and contain much of the information still available about the Wild West, even though some of that information was exaggerated to assure good ticket sales.

The advertising cars carried a manager and contracting agent who rented billboard space, contacted newspapers about the impending arrival of the show, and arranged the route for all three cars. Each car had a boss billposter, who arranged the work schedule and decided what posters to place where. There also was a boss banner man in each car, who arranged for the placement of banners in the town and on the show grounds. The workmen, or billposters, were further divided into teams, each with its own crew chief.

This type of organization was followed in every department of the Wild West. There was a general management figure in charge of several departments (or of similar activities in several departments), a department head in charge of each specific area, and other minor officials within the department where needed. Even the performers were divided into groups, each with its designated leader (usually called chiefs).

The system was highly successful because it allowed for the grueling one-a-day stand schedule that the Wild West followed and produced a healthy profit for most of the years it was in existence. The show went up, came down, and moved on with a minimum of effort because everyone had a specific job and a specific boss to refer problems to. Cody and his various partners always knew exactly where they stood financially, and the public was always well informed about the show's activities.

CHAPTER SIX

MESSAGES AND MEANINGS

Analyzing a performance of Buffalo Bill's Wild West is a difficult task. The first problem, the fact that the Wild West no longer exists and cannot be observed in production, means that the analysis must be more general and problematic than analyses of contemporary popular culture events. However, film fragments, pictures, and descriptions of the show do exist and some useful conclusions can be reached by careful study of these materials.

The second problem in analyzing a Wild West performance is the absence of a written text. But each individual act, and the performance as a whole, had a semiotic text that can be reconstructed at least partially from the information that still survives about the performances. Such a reconstruction is useful in helping to understand the types of messages that the show sent forth and the impact of these messages on the audience.

The third major problem in undertaking an analysis of this type is choosing which "performance" to analyze, as the show changed considerably over the 30 years it was presented. Many of the acts had a similar structure, however, and the most useful approach seems to be an analysis of each of the types of acts and then an analysis of the overall pattern of these events when they were combined into a program.

The basic physical element of the Wild West was a central, isolated oval space surrounded by seating for the audience on three sides, and a canvas wall with scenery painted on it on the fourth side. This space was neutral and was given meaning by the objects and performers it contained at any given time. The performance, and indeed each segment of the performance, was confined to a definite space and a definite length of time.

A performer in the Wild West who appeared in the arena with the intent of entertaining an audience was performing an act of communication that can be analyzed using the following model.

1. The *sender* or addresser was a single performer or a group of performers.
2. The *message* was whatever was performed by the performer(s).
3. The *receiver* or addressee was the audience, which followed and understood what was going on in the arena and gave signs of its appreciation.
4. A *context*: the act was a part of a particular program that took place in an institution (the Wild West) that was a part of some society.
5. A *contact*: the artist was careful to maintain contact between himself and the audience by clearly articulating his act and by exhibiting social behavior that acknowledged the reactions of the spectators, i.e., the feedback.
6. A *code*: this code follows the first three elements. Understanding a message presupposes that the receiver shares with the sender a knowledge of a system of rules of the type: x stands for y in context z.[1]

The message of the Wild West was communicated through several channels, sometimes all at once and sometimes one at a time. The show used visual, auditory, olfactory, and even tactile channels to get its messages across to the audience. For instance, during "The Attack on the Deadwood Stage" an audience member saw gunsmoke, smelled gunpowder, heard gunfire, was aware of the spectators nearest to him, as well as those across the arena from him, and a few audience members even experienced the tactile sensation of actually riding in the stage.

There were several different elements or classes of constituents at work in any given act of the Wild West:

1. *Linguistic messages*: a written one (which appeared on posters and/or in the program) and an oral one (the announcement of the act by the one who presented the show; projected words; Buffalo Bill's introduction).
2. *Social behavior* of the performer as he entered the arena, during the act, between sequences of the act, and as he left.

3. *The performer's costume*, which had been chosen from several possibilities.

4. *The accessories* the performer used and the style of decoration.

5. *The technical behavior* of the performer during the act.

6. *The music* played during the act.

7. *The lighting effects.*

8. *Linguistic behavior* for clown acts.

9. *Zoological components* for animal acts.

These constituents are the *subcodes* that form the *code* of a circus act's message, but with respect to the contextual culture, each of these constituents is a code (that is, clothing, music) that is a part of the *supercode* that constitutes the language we call "the circus" (which can be expanded to include the Wild West).[2]

The six types of Wild West acts, races, shooting acts, specialty acts, military exhibitions, riding and horse acts, and dramatic spectacles, each involved a series of choices made by the performer(s) to help communicate the message. These choices were not made randomly, but rather as a part of a system where one choice affected each of the others. Annie Oakley chose to have her husband and her dog as ring assistants, for instance. The basis of her act, or message to the audience, became one of normalcy and domesticity because of this choice. It then became reasonable for Annie to choose a costume that accentuated her role as the woman in her family; hence, she never wore trousers as part of the act. Even the choice of which tricks to perform was affected by this initial choice. During her act, Annie Oakley often shot objects that were in close proximity to members of her family (an apple on the dog's head, a dime between her husband's fingers), which helped to accentuate the absolute trust that should be a part of any family group.

The absence of a written text has been mentioned as a problem in the analysis of the Wild West. To overcome this problem the idea of a performance text must be explored. Performance text is defined by Keir Elam as "a macro-sign produced *in* the theatre (not *for* it) whose meaning is constituted by its total effect."[3] In other words, the performance of the written word is what carries the message to the audience. Such factors as lighting, sound, picturization, and body postures are important as a part of this process. Paul Bouissac further clarifies this concept when he says,

The concept of *text* cannot be restricted to a type of linguistic performance, either oral or written, because what constitutes a message as a text does not depend on the particular system within a given medium, but rather on formal properties, some of which pertain to the situation or context of the message, some to its constitutive structure.

He goes on to summarize these properties as follows:

1. Clear-cut boundaries that isolate a message as such, i.e., nonambiguous formal marks that delimit a finite set of interwoven meaningful elements.
2. A direct or indirect endurance over time, which makes it possible to "read" a message again and again . . . the possibility of repetition is ensured because the material of the message is invariable or because it is possible to memorize it exactly.
3. A deep system of relations ensuring the surface coherence of the message, in other words, a structure that accounts for its understandability, i.e., the possibility of building up from its elements a network of relations that includes all the actual terms as well as their relations.[4]

The Wild West most definitely had a performance text that exhibited these formal properties. The overall performance had a definite beginning and ending, marked by music and the spoken word (the orator's announcements). Also each act was introduced and had a definite ending. The audience was given clear signals in each case as to which set of elements constituted a message.

Wild West acts also endured over time. The material of each message remained constant from one performance to the next—the performers memorized their acts and performed them in the same way day after day—and even from one year to the next. "The Attack on the Deadwood Stage" remained virtually the same regardless of who was driving the coach, leading the Indians, or galloping to the rescue. The audience would always read the same message.

It is the third category that is the most interesting in examining the Wild West. The deep system of relations necessary to give each act its meaning was carefully built up through the advertising, programs, orator's remarks, and from act to act. The main elements of the Wild West were horses, guns, heroes, and villains. Each act made use of at least one of these elements and the most complex of them used all four. The basic messages being related were those of patriotism and expansionism (or the conquering of a wild and seemingly unwilling territory).

The name of the show, "Buffalo Bill's Wild West and Congress of Rough Riders of the World," gave a solid foundation for the structure of the show. The name of the hero (already established through books and plays) was placed first. The first part of the name (Buffalo) is somewhat exotic and evocative of another time and place, while the second part (Bill) is normal and familiar. This name was followed by the term "Wild West" which carried with it the promise of excitement and all the associations the audience had for Western America (including guns and horses). Next came the mention of a "Congress," meaning "group" but carrying with it many patriotic connotations, followed by "Rough Riders," again promising excitement, and more specifically horses. The final tag "of the World" carried the expectation of the audience beyond the boundaries of their own country to an even grander expectation of things they may never have seen or heard.

The title was prominently displayed on all posters and other advertising and was supported by graphics that introduced the gun and the villain to the audience. These graphic pictures also featured horses prominently and often set up the relationship of hero versus villain. Add to these newspaper articles about Cody's career in the West as a buffalo hunter and scout, and the audience was well prepared to understand the performance text as it was presented to them.

The performance began with the band playing "The Star Spangled Banner." This music helped remind the crowd that the Wild West was definitely an American entertainment. Though this song was not yet the national anthem, it was well known as a military tune, and the words express strong patriotic sentiments. It was followed by the introduction of the performers on their horses. This established one relationship of people to horses (people definitely dominant, with horses used as tools), and emphasized the division of each group from the others, and each group's individual character. If the exact order of entrance were known, some idea of the relative importance of the groups and their relationship to one another might be gained, but this information no longer exists. All that is certain is that a group of Indians entered first and Colonel Cody entered last. It seems clear that this relationship helped to emphasize both Cody's dominance over the Indians (and other performers) in his show, and on another level, the white man's dominance over all Indians.

Buffalo Bill's entrance had an important part in establishing the structure of meaning for the rest of the show. He appeared riding alone and was given hero status in this way. He performed in a carefully chosen costume on a carefully chosen horse that was equally carefully costumed. Cody galloped into the arena, accompanied by the announcement of his full name, clearly showing his dominance of the animal he rode and his skill in riding horses. He came to a quick stop, swept off his hat (both to show his understanding of the social norms of polite behavior and to make himself more visible), and both he and his horse bowed to the audience. Again Cody demonstrated his control of the horse, and a new element or type of relationship was introduced. The horse was humanized by this action, and it became clear that on certain occasions horse and rider could become a team, accomplishing tasks together. A friendship or mutual respect between animal and rider was implied by this action and was reinforced at various points in the program.

After the bow had been executed, Cody spoke a phrase. As far as I can determine, these were the only words spoken by a performer (other than the orator) to the audience as a part of the show. This action again isolated Cody as the leader of the group and as the controlling figure of the Wild West. The phrase, "Ladies and gentlemen, allow me to present to you a Congress of Rough Riders of the World," emphasized Cody's understanding of polite social behavior (once again separating him from the barbaric Wild West image) and reinforced the associations already held by the audience by repeating a key part of the title of the show.

Photographs reveal that Cody had several favorite horses that he rode in the show between 1883 and 1913. Not all of them were white, but several were, and most of the poster material shows him mounted on a white horse. Whatever color the horse was, it was always decked out for the opening of the show in a special headstall and breastband that had gold pieces in the shape of flowers and cloverleaves attached to them. The overall appearance was that of simple elegance. The special rigging was not glamorous or ornate but was different enough to stand out. These trappings were sometimes removed for Cody's later appearances and replaced with a more ordinary bit and bridle. The horse's mane and tail seem never to have been braided. They were left to flow naturally. This helped emphasize the idea that the horse had once been wild and, while it had been tamed and ridden by Buffalo Bill, it had not had its wild spirit broken.

Cody's costume for this opening number consisted of a fringed and beaded leather shirt that for the audience probably had associations with the scout and plainsman figures of the dime novel and suggested a relationship with the Indians; leather gauntlets, at least sometimes beaded; hip-high black leather boots; and a white or light-colored Stetson hat. His overall appearance was enhanced by his long, flowing hair (left as wild and untamed as his horse's mane) and his goatee and moustache (which were carefully trimmed, possibly to show that he could associate with polite society as well as Indians and soldiers). Pictures also reveal that Buffalo Bill sometimes changed into a plainer, fabric shirt for his shooting act.

Once Cody had made his announcement, the riders galloped off into the maze figure which mixed the riders of all the nations and of both sexes into a whirling mass of color. Cody did not participate in this maneuver; he sat on his horse and watched his performers, again a controlling figure and an isolated hero.

The order of the rest of the program varied from year to year, and many of the acts were similar to one another. For these reasons I will concentrate on the messages of each type of act, using examples from specific events as they apply. The six categories of events are races, shooting acts, specialty acts, military exhibitions, riding and horse acts, and dramatic spectacles.

The racing events used two of the major elements of the Wild West. Most obviously, the horse was featured, and every race that was run had a winner who was, at least briefly, a hero. Several types of relationships were established by the racing events. First of all, there was the relationship of the rider to the animal being ridden. On a continuum of horse as tool and rider as absolute ruler, to horse as a person's companion and person as friend of horse, the racing events fall almost dead center. Person and animal had to work together to win the race (the horse being humanized by the audience's assumption that it wanted to win) and to overcome the obstacles put in their way (hurdles, posts, a special gymkhana course). But the rider sometimes forced the animal to extra effort with spur and whip and in some cases made animals untrained for jumping leap hurdles. The person was always the rider and the horse always the tool used to accomplish a task. This message was further emphasized by the race between an Indian on a horse and an Indian on foot. The course was arranged in such a way that the Indian on foot always won. Human superiority to the horse was reinforced quite strongly by this act.

The complex relationship of person to horse was further explored by featuring riders of different nationalities with their native mounts and riding gear. While the person remained the ruler, various levels of sophistication were shown. The Indian rode bareback (an almost wild horse ridden by an equally wild person), the cowboy rode in the Western saddle (a working man with his most valuable piece of equipment), the Western girls rode astride (unrefined women showing their rough upbringing), and the English gentleman rode an English jumping saddle (a highly sophisticated man in complete control of his animal with almost no equipment).

Besides the relationship of person to horse, these races pointed out relationships between nationalities. Both "The International Race" and "The Relay Race" pitted riders of different nationalities against one another. The riders were costumed in their native dress (or the Wild West's best approximation of it), and the horses were rigged in native bridles and saddles, so that the audience could clearly identify the various nationalities. There is no evidence that these races were rigged in any way. Apparently, the fastest horse and the best rider won. It seems to have been more important for the audience to see the nationalities striving against one another in a fair contest than it was for them to see a particular nationality victorious. After all, these riders had all been gathered together by an American hero, and they were appearing in a distinctly American entertainment. Any foreign rider winning a race within this framework posed no threat and in fact may have made the audience congratulate themselves on their sense of fair play (especially since they were allowed to cheer on an American rider).

The sharpshooting acts were about guns and people's relationship to guns. The skill of the performer became the major focus of these acts. It did not matter if the performer was male or female, big or small, old or young, as long as he or she could shoot with great accuracy. These guns never were used directly as instruments of violence. They were used to shoot highly visible objects like glass balls or apples, or to shoot almost invisibly small objects (further proving the shooter's skill) like coins or marbles, but never to kill living things. The direct message of guns as safe objects used for sport was reinforced by the appearance of women (Annie Oakley and Lillian Smith), children (Johnny Baker—The Cowboy Kid, and Baby Ray Ellis—Cody's sometime ring assistant), and family groups (Annie Oakley and her husband, Captain Bogardus and his four sons) in these acts.

But the violent nature of guns was not totally absent even from these acts. Part of the thrill of seeing an apple shot off a poodle's head lies in the fear that the poodle may be killed. This holds true in any act where an assistant is in danger if the performer is not sufficiently skilled. The obvious shattering of a target was another reminder of the power of the firearms. Glass balls were broken in huge numbers at the Wild West. The audience must have been aware that anything that could break a glass target flying through the air could also kill live targets in a similar manner. Added to the impact of seeing an object shattered was the visual message of flame and smoke, and the aural message of the report each time a gun was fired. These factors also were strong reminders of the power of firearms. Occasionally audience members may even have been spattered by shot from the shells discharged in these events, further reminding them that guns had a deadly use as well as a sporting one.

The violent uses of guns were also alluded to in Cody's solo shooting act. Buffalo Bill often used an Indian assistant to gallop around the arena with him, throwing glass balls for him to shoot. This relationship had various connotations. First, there was the message that the Indian was the helper and Cody the star. The audience received this message in several ways. The program mentioned only Cody as a performer in this act, and the orator probably announced only the name of the act ("Colonel W. F. Cody [Buffalo Bill] and his unique feats of sharpshooting while riding at full speed"). But it was the visual part of the message that firmly established Cody's dominance. The Indian rode carrying a basket full of glass balls, which he threw into the air one at a time. Cody rode beside and slightly behind him, carrying a rifle which he fired regularly. This picture left no room for doubt about who was in control in this relationship (and by association, in all white/Indian relationships).

The events I have categorized as specialty events were quite different from both the races and the sharpshooting events. They featured groups or individual performers with unique talents. While some of these acts tended to resemble circus acts in their structure and performance, others were displays of distinctly Western skills. A few of the acts were traditional circus events adapted to the Wild West by choice of costumes and animals.

The strictly Western events included "Roping Wild Texas Steers," "Roping and Riding Wild Bison," "The Pony Express," and "Mexican Joe" (lasso expert). The roping events allowed the cowboys to exhibit their horsemanship and their skill in overcoming "wild" animals. The relationship between rider and horse was that of a team working together to conquer a foe. There was a hierarchy established in these acts with man at the top, followed by the domesticated horses, with the wild steers or buffalo at the bottom. This hierarchy could be upset by one of the men being thrown from one of the animals (either his own horse, or a steer or buffalo), but such an occurrence probably served to convince the audience of the difficulty of the task, and amplified the message of dominance when a cowboy (either the one who was thrown or another) mounted and rode the recalcitrant animal. If the animal was not finally subjected to the man's will, the audience received a message that this show was indeed the Wild West and that there were untameable elements within it.

Little is known about Mexican Joe's act, but it seems related to juggling acts in the circus. The object of a rope act is to keep a loop revolving in the air while the performer does things that make this feat difficult (jumping in and out of the loop, adding a second rope, spinning guns at the same time he spins the rope), just as the object of a juggling act is to keep objects revolving in the air while the performer works to make the task more difficult (adding more objects, standing on his head, standing on one leg). In each case, the act is highly intelligible to the audience because of its high visibility and its clear structure. The performer is identified (by the orator or ringmaster), and he survives or completes a series of tasks that are increasingly difficult—the last task being of such a magnitude that the performer attains hero status.[5]

"The Pony Express" had a very definite narrative structure. The rider appeared, galloped around the arena, changed horses, and galloped off again. The horse and rider were definitely a team, and the carrier of the U.S. Mail was shown as a skilled horseman who spared no time in making his appointed ride. In some cases the exchange of horses was made more complex by the addition of a cabin and other performers to hold the horses and help the rider on his way. The cabin was painted to resemble rough-hewn logs, the station master carried a rifle in one hand and the mail pouch in the other, and the additional performers were all costumed as cowboys. The presence of the cowboys ready to ride to the rescue and the rifle of the station master helped send a message to the audience that the mail carrier was always in danger, but even in the "Wild West" where dwellings were crude, the U.S. Mail would be protected, and the mail carrier had friends ready to help him.

The most obvious circus act included in the Wild West was the "Arab Acrobats." Pictures show that this troupe performed several feats simultaneously in different parts of the arena. They were dressed in costumes totally different from any of the Western costumes or from any of the other riding costumes. Their costumes were dark-colored tunics with light-colored cloth sewn on them in geometric patterns, short pants, high socks, and low-cut shoes. On the center of each tunic just below the performer's chin were the shapes of a star and a half-moon. While some of the performers did fairly familiar acrobatic feats like building human pyramids, and walking a tightrope, others were doing much more exotic things like fencing in the Far Eastern style and spinning like a Whirling Dervish. Both the choice of activities and the choice of costumes accentuated the differences between these performers and those performers representing Americans. None of the four major elements of the Wild West appeared in this act. The only connection the act seems to have had with the rest of the show was that it showed another group of people performing supposedly native activities (like the Cossacks, Gauchos, and Filipinos).

Three specialty acts took their inspiration from similar circus acts. "Indian from Africa," "Cowboy Cyclist," and "High Jumping Contest" were all adaptations of activities seen regularly in the circus. In the first, an exotic animal (in this case an elk) was saddled and bridled and ridden around the arena by a black man. The title of the act linked the black man with the American Indians in the show and carried a clear message about the wild and exotic nature of both peoples.

The "Cowboy Cyclist" jumped his bicycle over a space 56 feet wide. Similar in intent to the circus acts featuring human cannonballs, daring motorcycle jumps, or performers diving into a small tank of water, this act pitted a performer against seemingly gigantic odds, which he overcame to gain hero status. The announcement in the program that the performer would not jump in high winds or heavy rains made the task seem even more difficult. By choosing a cowboy title and costume, the performer linked himself to the Wild West theme, and his bicycle had enough of the properties of a horse to be linked with one in the minds of the audience.

The "High Jumping Contest" combined several elements of the circus. The performer's competition were a dog and two horses. These animals had to be trained to complete the tasks set for them without appearing to be controlled by the performer. This was necessary to make the contest seem fair. An animal under a trainer's control can be ordered to miss a jump.

An animal who is free to choose will miss a jump because it cannot complete the task. The audience saw what appeared to be a fair contest won by the human performer. The performer had asserted not only his mental superiority (by getting the animals to compete in the first place) but his biological superiority (by winning the contest fair and square). This type of dominance is asserted in many traditional circus acts such as those featuring cats, bears, and performing horses.

The specialty act that does not seem to fit into either a strictly circus structure or a structure based on Western skills is "Football on Horseback." This act was set up more like a sporting event and was similar in structure to the racing events. Two mounted teams—cowboys and Indians—were pitted against each other in a struggle to move a huge leather ball down the field and into the opposing team's goal. Each horse and rider seemed to work as a team in this act, although the horses actually had no wish to win the contest but merely followed the instructions of their riders. The teams were carefully chosen to point up the battle between white man and Indian, and the performers wore costumes clearly chosen to make it easy for the audience to see which team was which. The leather ball that was used was six feet in diameter. The huge size allowed the audience to follow the game clearly from anywhere in the grandstand and helped to emphasize the size of the horses and their riders. (If the ball had to be this big to provide a challenge to the performers, then the horses and riders must be huge indeed.) As with the races there is no evidence that this event was rigged. The contest was played to its natural conclusion at each performance. If the Indians won, the audience received a message of fair play and mutual respect between the participants. If the cowboys won, the message of fair play still remained, but the message of dominance and superiority was added.

"Auto Polo" was an event that was added to the show for the last season. This type of event was seen in circuses of the period, and in fact such modern circus acts as unicycle basketball are closely related. The focus was shifted from cowboys and Indians to the novelty of the motor car and its capabilities and to the daring of the men who stood on the running boards and batted a polo ball around the arena. There apparently was a contest between teams to get the ball into the opposite goal, but the real objective was to show off all the things a car could do, and to help audience members substitute the concept of a car for that of a horse (as they were having to do in their everyday lives).

Military exhibitions were the fourth type of act in Buffalo Bill's Wild West. Only the names of most of these acts have survived, but descriptions and pictures of three events ("Artillery Drill," "Aurora Zouaves," and "Life-Saving Drill") give some idea of the general message and structure of this type of act. The respectability of military service, the preparedness and skill of the troops, and their complete knowledge of equipment were all emphasized by the military events.

The "Artillery Drill" was a demonstration of how horse-drawn artillery pieces were transported, prepared for firing, and fired in the field. The performers (all actual military men) were dressed in U.S. military uniforms and the exhibition was carried out with great speed, as if an actual battle were in progress. The horses in this act were simply tools to get the guns in place. Once the guns had been fired, they were prepared for transportation once again and moved out of the arena. Several times performers were wounded by the premature discharge of a cannon, and the audience was reminded that military men daily risk their lives for their country—even when there is no enemy present.

The "Life-Saving Drill" emphasized the military's role in protecting civilians from natural disasters. Again this act was done with great speed and showed the extreme dexterity of the men in the Life-Saving Service in setting up and using their equipment to save lives. Because of the narrative structure of this act, the performers gained hero status by overcoming the storm and the danger of the shipwreck to rescue the crew of the ship. But without the equipment and its careful manipulation, nothing could have been done to save the crew of the sinking ship. The act supported "The Artillery Drill" in its message about the military's need for, and reliance on, mechanical devices.

The last military event that has been clearly described is "The Aurora Zouaves." The purpose of this act was to exhibit the usefulness of a national militia. The double-time quick-march maneuvers executed by these civilians, dressed in quasi-military uniforms, made a strong statement to the audience. Not only did civilians have the right to bear arms, but they had the opportunity to learn to use them well. If this group of normal American men could learn to march, handle rifles, and scale walls with such precision, any American male should be able to perform just as well. Another part of the message of this act was the patriotic pride and sense of security that was engendered by knowing American civilians could be trained to such perfection without ever joining the Army. If the militia was needed, it would serve with distinction.

Events involving riding and horses were numerous in the Wild West. Not only were audiences quite familiar with horses as a part of their everyday lives, but they had been treated to early circuses that featured horse acts almost exclusively. The horse act was so popular because "equestrian performers took an ordinary, everyday experience and raised it to the level of art. Audiences then fully realized just how difficult it was for the riders to control their horses and their own bodies so completely and effortlessly that the two figures merged into a single graceful form."[6] There were three types of riding events in the show: the Rough Riders of the World, fancy riding and trick horses, and Western activities. Each of these types of acts established or reinforced different relationships between people and horses.

The sequences featuring the Rough Riders began as individual events set apart from each other in the program. The Russian Cossacks, South American Gauchos, and Mexicans each had a segment to themselves. During the period when the acts were presented in this way, the individual groups were given special attention and so gained a certain dignity and implied importance. This arrangement of the program also set the foreign performers apart from the more American portions of the show and even separated the groups from one another. This separation made it clear to the audience that while these riders were skilled and interesting, they were not a part of the American Western movement that was being glorified by the show.

In all three acts, the horse was a tool of locomotion, and while the rider and horse might have seemed to be a team, the emphasis in this relationship was on the rider's skill at staying on the horse, and not the horse itself. The riders in each group executed daring tricks to show their complete ease in the saddle, and the audience was able to understand this message quite well because of the society's overall dependence on, and knowledge of, horses.

Each act also communicated a message of cohesion within the group that was performing. The Russians sang and danced together, as well as executing complicated military formations that relied for their success on the teamwork of the group. Apparently, the Gauchos also sang a national song at their entrance, and their act featured the teamwork involved in South American ranching techniques. The Mexicans worked as a group to make their leader, Vincenti Oropeza, stand out in at least one portion of their act. While Oropeza performed his lasso act, the other performers became riding and walking targets for his spinning loop. Oropeza would lasso four running horses and riders with one loop, or a man and a horse would jump through a loop provided by the leader.

By 1895 these acts had begun to be combined in a single event entitled "Ten Minutes with the Rough Riders of the World." As the years passed, this time limit was gradually cut down until the event lasted only three minutes, and the message to the audience changed. They saw all the foreign performers at one time, isolated from the American performers but not from one another. The importance and individual dignity of each group was diminished, and the boundaries between groups established only by their costumes and relative positions in the arena. (Unfortunately, these positions are no longer known.) The audience members were further hampered in receiving a clear message by the large number of signals being sent during an act with this many performers, costumes, and activities. Each section of the audience would have had one group nearer to them than the others, and they probably concentrated their attention on that part of the event to help cut down the interference in receiving a message. In this way the individual dignity of each group was diminished, as was the audience's exposure to the unique character of several foreign cultures.

The fancy riding acts were quite different from the Rough Riding events. These acts were similar to circus acts featuring trained horses and emphasized the human qualities of horses and the skill of the performers who trained them. In these acts the attention of the audience was centered on the horses and their abilities, rather than on the trainer, who received his recognition indirectly through the audience's approval of the tasks the horses could complete. These tasks involved bowing, jumping, and cantering in time to music, standing on their hind legs, and kneeling down. Sometimes the horses were bridled and saddled and actually ridden during the events, and sometimes they appeared with no trappings (as in a circus Liberty Horse Act). The costumes of the horses and performers were chosen to link the acts with the Wild West theme, and the color of the horses that appeared probably was carefully regulated (as is done in standard circus practice[7]).

One of the riding events that exhibited Western riding activities was closely related to the fancy riding acts. The "Virginia Reel on Horseback" had trained horses, probably in matched pairs, that participated with their riders in a Western dance. This event placed more focus on the rider and horse as a team than did the other fancy riding acts, but the horses were obviously performing tasks that required careful training and received more attention than horses in the Rough Riding events. These horses also were humanized by their participation in the human social event called dancing.

Besides the relationship of person to horse, this event reinforced the relationship of man to woman, or more specifically, of cowboy to cowgirl. The performers in this act paired off and went through the motions of a well-known dance figure. The message received by the audience was one of normalcy and security (a familiar social relationship) mixed with a feeling of the exotic (horses had been added). Once again the Wild West managed to show that its members understood the proper social behavior of the time but were not completely ruled by that understanding.

Quite different in some respects from the other Wild West horse acts, "Cowboy Fun" presented horses in two ways. During the part of the act where the cowboys exhibited their trick riding skills, the horses were shown in much the same way as they were in the Rough Riding events. But during the bronco riding part of the act, horses became wild, mean animals to be conquered (villains), and the cowboys became skilled, strong men who could conquer them (heroes).

The wildness of the horses was shown when they were turned into the arena with no riders and no one holding their reins, by the way they were lassoed and then held down by several men (emphasizing the horse's strength and size), by their extreme behavior when they were mounted, and by the fact that a rider rarely rode a horse to a standstill, but was either bucked off or leaped off when the ride got too difficult.

The performers in this act gained their hero status in several ways. First, the relative sizes of the combatants was clearly shown by having the cowboys and cowgirls appear in the arena on foot (the only time these performers did so) instead of mounted on tamed horses, while the horses appeared fully equipped with saddles and bridles (making them appear even larger). Second, it always took more than one man to hold the horse while a single person mounted, but that single individual did mount the horse even in the face of such great odds. Once the horse was mounted, a contest ensued that usually ended with the horse as victor (or only temporarily dominated). But the rider had shown a willingness to risk the ride and had shown his or her skills at riding by staying mounted at all. The presence of so many tame horses with the show testified to the perseverance and bravery of anyone who made a living at taming such wild beasts for other people's use.

Both men and women performed in this act, and while there were more men than women, a definite message was sent to the audience that Western women were strong, brave individuals who did their share of work on the Western frontier. It must be remembered, however, that the act was never performed exclusively by women and that the women did not help to hold horses for other riders, but only rode the broncs. In this way certain social norms were given credence—men should help women to subdue wild beasts, women should not undertake tasks requiring brute strength, and even that women should be helped to mount their horses.

The most complicated events in the Wild West were the dramatic spectacles. The content of these spectacles varied from generic Western events, to specific historic events, to current events, to exotic pageants. Each event was told in broad pantomime, followed a narrative structure, and made use of most, if not all, of the arena. Certain real items appeared as props in these spectacles and so gained special significance, and elaborate descriptions of the actual events on which the acts were based were included in the program.

There were many details that helped to separate one spectacle from another (a stagecoach versus covered wagons, or a settler's cabin), but the structure and the messages were similar. Each event began with some action to help set the scene. For instance, the Indians appeared and set up camp, the horse thief limped into the camp of a sleeping cowboy, or the soldiers bivouacked at the base of San Juan Hill. Then a period of relative peace would ensue, during which the performers further established time and place by performing actions typical of the characters they portrayed. Songs were sung around the campfire, Indian war dances were performed, or the stagecoach was driven safely around the arena. This period of peace was disturbed by some action that alerted the audience to the action that was to follow: an army scout spied on the Indian camp, an Indian spied on the wagon train or cabin, the buffalo appeared in the arena and went to the "spring" for a drink, for example.

These parts of the message were clear and no more complex than messages already sent to and received by the audience. The relationships of people to guns, people to horses, men to women, and racial groups to one another were clearly established in these two steps and would not change as the act progressed. In this way the audience was prepared for the more frantic and complicated message that was to follow.

Once the two opposing camps had been established clearly and the link between the two had been revealed, the spectacles speeded up and spread out. Instead of a steadily paced, single-action pantomime, the audience was suddenly presented with a fast-paced, multiaction battle sequence. These sequences featured many performers, much gunsmoke, lots of horses, and a great deal of noise. No one held still for very long in these sequences, and focus was not directed to any one spot. But the spectators knew that those performers earlier established as the heroes (or good guys) would ultimately defeat the villains (or bad guys) and so could enjoy the grand scope of this part of the spectacles without becoming confused by it. (Even in the case of "Custer's Last Fight" the audience knew the Indians would win and so could follow the action.)

The final stages of these spectacles mirrored the opening sequences. The battle frenzy would die down as the heroes vanquished the foe, there would be a period of peace while the wounded were helped from the field, and finally the performers would remove any remaining props (teepees, guns, the cabin) in character.

The audience was aided in understanding these spectacles by a description of the action in the program. These programs also pointed out the historical significance of certain props (notably the Deadwood Stage). The use of an actual object to represent that class of object in a reenactment of a specific event made the act seem that much more real. The stagecoach or wagon (or for that matter the person) had been through this event in the real world, and the event in the Wild West was imbued with all the glory and excitement of the actual event by the presence of the object in the reenactment for the show. This was true of the addition of any detail from an actual battle that was well-known to the audience (singing "There'll Be a Hot Time in the Old Town Tonight" during "The Battle of San Juan Hill," for instance).

The overall structure of the show changed a great deal over the years between 1883 and 1913. The opening and closing sequences remained the same, and certain acts like Annie Oakley's and "The Attack on the Settler's Cabin" remained in similar positions when they were presented, but few programs were exactly alike. Whatever factors controlled the selection and ordering of acts, it is clear that they were not placed randomly. It seems obvious that certain rules concerning the rhythm, build, and interest of the program were followed, but exactly how these decisions were reached is unknown.[8]

There is much analysis still to be done on the details of each individual event, and I propose the above as a model for studying how each act was structured and presented. A great deal of specific information has yet to be found about many of these events. Questions about the specific music played during the events, the specific words of the orator, the positioning of certain acts and performers, and the ebb and flow of the overall performance may never be answered. But new information is continually being discovered about Buffalo Bill's Wild West, and eventually further semiotic analysis may be possible.

CHAPTER SEVEN

FINAL IMPRESSIONS

Wyoming.
Oh! West, of West!

Land of a man who as a boy was a mighty pioneer in the development of a new world. Rider, intrepid, audacious, simple, unconscious wild western country boy of the Pony Express, William Cody, Buffalo Bill master of the hunt, charmed against harm, loved and trusted by the Indians. Buffalo Bill who made the old world know what it was, the wild of West, a link between the old world and the new. Buffalo Bill, a master of picturesque beauty and grandeur, from Wyoming, a great country which has stood side by side with its sister-States in the great sacrifices for victory. I have to come to you one day.[1]

—Marie, Queen of Rumania

While there is no way to measure accurately the impact of the Wild West on its audiences or its influence in the creation of the myth of the American West, such testimonies as the one above give some clue as to the strength of the effect of the show on audience members. There is no doubt that new fashions were begun, new foods introduced to Europeans, and new Western character-types presented to audiences by the Wild West. But the overall production, which was billed as genuine and authentic, soon transcended its intention of representing the contemporary Western scene and created a West based largely on illusion.

The West that Cody wished to portray had passed into history by the time his show became a success. The Indian battles, lonely frontier cabins, and the Pony Express were all events of the past and had little to do with the ongoing process of making the West a functioning part of the United States. Nonetheless, these events were a part of the very recent past and had a great appeal for audiences. The very fact that the frontier had disappeared was one of the reasons why so many people found the Wild West fascinating.

Nostalgia was a common feeling, as the existence of the boundless land for the taking, which had been the frontier's greatest treasure, was now a thing of the past. . . . Now that the rugged and adventurous frontier life as epitomized by the cowboy on the open range was jeopardized, it was natural that it be not only dramatized, but analyzed, as each man in his own way sought to clarify the nature of what it was that was disappearing.[2]

Cody and members of his company had been present at many of the historically significant battles and other events of the 1800s and had lived through the day-to-day business of taming the frontier, but the restrictions of theatrical production, including a limited playing space, problems of transporation, and the demands of making messages clear and understandable, transformed this authentic knowledge of actual events into a representation of generic Western incidents. Because of this transformation, audiences saw cowboys without cows, Indians without buffalo, battles where help always arrived in the nick of time, and guns that never killed anyone. The whole bloody and arduous task of taming an unsettled land was romanticized and glorified and the moral questions that that settlement entailed were glossed over and ignored.

In this way the authentic characters, props, and moments in the show were indiscriminately mixed with the romanticized version of life in the West, and the audience received an impression that reflected this mixture. They saw both a fairly accurate example of a Pony Express ride and a totally fictitious ending to the Custer massacre (showing Buffalo Bill's arrival at the battlefield) with no way to distinguish truth from fiction. The end result was the addition of new components to the myth of the American West which had been partially formed already by dime novels, melodramas, the brochures and lectures of the land speculators, and the accounts of those who had traveled and lived in the West. The addition of the Wild West to these other sources of myth caused changes in each form and changed the overall myth as well.

Buffalo Bill himself has become a part of this myth. Many of the actual incidents of his life have been romanticized and glorified by so many different writers, movie makers, and playwrights that, even when the truth of an incident has been proven, it cannot supplant the story that has grown up around it. Although it is known that Cody killed the Indian chief Yellow Hair in the midst of an ongoing battle, for instance, the story of a hand-to-hand duel between the lines of two patiently waiting forces still persists in biographies, movies, and children's books.

Cody was the principal source of many of these stories. Not only did he write four full-length, highly exciting (though not highly accurate) books about himself, but he also allowed his press agents to write inaccurate histories of his life for programs and couriers and sold his sister's romanticized biography, *The Last of the Scouts*, on the show grounds. He also starred in melodramas supposedly depicting actual events in his life, featured spectacles in his Wild West based on battles in which he had fought, and made movies about these same events and battles. While all these dramatizations were based on fact, they were embellished and changed to make them more dramatic and exciting.

Another source of misinformation or exaggeration was the hundreds of dime novels written by many different authors that featured Buffalo Bill. Similar in their effect were the colorful and numerous show posters that depicted Cody vanquishing Indians, saving passengers from stagecoach robbers, and leading people into the promised land. The novels created the impression of a man who could handle any problem, defeat any foe, and win any bet. The posters did nothing to discourage this notion and were, in fact, general enough in the events they depicted to support these notions rather than change them.

Friends and relatives added to the myth by repeating and exaggerating Buffalo Bill's stories, both during his lifetime and after his death. Both his sister and his wife wrote biographies; Johnny Baker started a museum and gave lectures about Cody; and members of his troupe wrote stories about their years in the

Wild West. All these were based on some grain of truth, but none were careful, accurate chronicles of Cody's life. Also adding to the myth were Cody's enemies and debunkers. These people were responsible for the stories that Cody slaughtered buffalo indiscriminately, was always drunk, and was a terrible business-man. These stories, too, have a grain of truth, but are no more accurate than the ones glorifying Cody.

Movies, television programs, books, articles, poems, plays, and comic books about Buffalo Bill Cody have continued to appear since his death. A glance through the references in this book will give some idea of the wealth of written material about Cody, but it does not reflect the wealth of visual material also available. For instance, between 1923 and 1976, 35 movies about Buffalo Bill were made, the most recent being Robert Altman's film of Arthur Kopit's *Indians*.[3] Many of these movies are standard Hollywood Westerns with Cody as the hero, but a few (especially Altman's film) try to return this mythical hero to the stature of a real man by questioning the myth and comparing what Cody stands for in the Western mythology with what he actually did on the Western frontier. But often these films merely play up the bad side of the myth instead of the good and never really reveal anything very accurate or interesting about Cody.

Whatever Cody's real life was like, it was the mythic figure that audiences loved and that we remember. The combination of his experience in the West, his vast personal charm, and his instinct for showmanship put him squarely in the public eye at a time when the American people were fascinated by the West. He became a symbol for all the best the frontier had to offer— the freedom, the excitement, and the heroism. While the truth about his life is interesting, it is the stories based on the truth that capture our imaginations and assure Cody a permanent place in the American consciousness.

Another important addition to the myth of the American West was the introduction of the character-type of the cowboy. This mythical figure also had a real counterpart who participated in the long drives of the 1850s and worked the ranches of the West when barbed wire made its appearance; but it was the Wild West that began the process of romanticizing the cowboy and giving him his mythic hero status.

Beginning in 1883, Cody featured "cow-boys" in the Wild West. They were shown roping Texas steers, roping and riding wild buffalo, and riding bucking horses. In later years they had an act to themselves ("Cowboy Fun"), and it was these performers who always rescued the stage, the settler's cabin, and the emigrant train from Indians. Leading the group in each of these activities was the chief of the cowboys. For the early years of the show this position was filled by Buck Taylor, who was billed as "King of the Cowboys." This man not only introduced the concept of a hero cowboy to audiences of the Wild West, but was made the central figure of a series of dime novels by writer Prentiss Ingram. The first novel of this series appeared in 1887 (three years after Taylor first appeared in Cody's show) and the sixth and last in 1891. These were not the first novels to have cowboy characters, but the first to make "one unusually gifted cowboy the hero of a series of related tales."[4] This tradition has been continued by cowboy movie heroes such as Roy Rogers and by television series such as *The Lone Ranger*.

These cowboy heroes did not spend their time herding cows in either the Wild West or the dime novel. They were portrayed as brave, strong men, the knights-errant of the plains, who were noble, generous, and always true to their word. They protected women in distress, punished wrongdoers, and made the West a safer place to live. The dull, dirty, back-breaking task of getting the cattle to market was transformed into a bold, colorful, individualistic way of life. Audiences and readers were not told about frostbite, dust storms, bad food, loneliness, and boredom; they saw men riding freely over the plains, making their own rules, and living their lives as they chose. This mythic figure took precedence over all other pioneer figures associated with the American frontier and came to exemplify the spirit and freedom of life in the West and finally, of life in America.

The Wild West also helped to introduce the figure of the pioneer woman into the myth of the American West. Along with a general trend in dime novel literature in the 1880s, Buffalo Bill featured certain women as something more than objects to be rescued.[5] As early as 1886, Annie Oakley received star billing as a sharpshooter, and Lillian Smith gained similar billing not long afterwards. By 1887 Georgia Duffy and Dell Ferrell were riding horse races in divided skirts, and that same year the first lady bronc rider appeared with the show. The term "cowgirl" was not coined until 1905 when it was applied to Lucille Mulhall, a rider with the 101 Ranch Show,[6] but the first Western heroines appeared long before this in dime novels, the melodrama, and the Wild West.

Not all the women in the Wild West were featured as female counterparts to the cowboy. In fact, only a very small number of the women with the show were portrayed this way. There were also the women of the emigrant train who needed to be protected, the women captives taken by the Indians who had to be rescued, and the pretty young ladies who rode the High School horses and performed in "The Virginia Reel on Horseback." Along with these, Indian women were shown moving and establishing their village (as well as torturing their white victims). Arab women were shown helping to entertain the captives in "The Far East—A Dream of the Orient," and little girls (Eva Mudge and Rose Ellis) were shown riding their ponies during various acts.

The heroine of the mythic West was never as clearly established as the hero. Perhaps it was too difficult to reconcile the need for someone for the hero to protect with the emerging realization that the women of the West had shared equally with the men the dangers and hardships of frontier life and had emerged quite able to protect themselves. Whatever the reason, both the genteel, passive woman who rode side saddle and needed protecting, and the competent, active woman who rode astride and took her place beside the cowboy, persisted in the dime novel and the Wild West, and it is these same types that we see perpetuated in modern movies and television programs.

The Indian was as important to the myth of the American West as the cowboy, and the Wild West had its part in shaping this mythic figure as well. The dime novel and other literature had already established the two principal types of Indians— noble savages and bloodthirsty barbarians—and the Wild West featured examples of both. In their village on the grounds and while running races or dancing "traditional" dances, the Indian was shown as a noble savage—different, primitive, but basically nonthreatening. But during the battle sequences he was depicted as a bloodthirsty barbarian—screaming, shooting, and better off vanquished or dead.

Cody did make some effort to allow his Indians dignity and recognition. The Indians were introduced in groups, each with a chief or leader who was announced by his title; Cody scheduled those events that showed the more noble (or perhaps more realistic) view of Indian life; and he took his Indians to plays and parties wherever he went to allow them greater visibility as people who could enjoy whatever kind of entertainment was offered them.

But the real contribution that Buffalo Bill's Wild West made to the mythic character of the Indian was the way it firmly established the Plains Indians as the symbol for all American Indians in the minds of an entire generation of Americans.

The very image we have of the American Indian—riding on his pony with feathered headdress—remains with us in Western novels, films, and television, because that was the kind of Indian, the Sioux, which Buffalo Bill's Wild West employed. Apaches wore no feathers and fought mostly on foot, but if they are to be believed as "Indians" in Western films they must get on a horse and put on their war bonnets because that's what we've become accustomed to.[7]

This portrayal of the Indian had more immediate effects upon its audience. An 1894 newspaper clipping reports that "some boys burned Charles Benney at the stake" after seeing the Wild West. The boy died from his wounds.[8] This was apparently not an isolated incident because in 1915 an Indian named Chauncy Yellow Robe wrote,

We see that the showman is manufacturing the Indian plays intended to amuse and instruct young children, and is teaching them that the Indian is only a savage being. We hear now and then of a boy or girl who is hurt playing savage. These are the direct consequences of the Wild West Indian shows and moving pictures that depict lawlessness and hatred.[9]

In fact, the overall portrayal of life in the West had a great impact on youngsters who witnessed the Wild West. On September 10, 1894, a boy shot his brother in the head while trying to copy a sharpshooting trick of Annie Oakley's. The bullet was removed, and a newspaper article expressed the hope that the boy would live.[10] Even when such emulation did not end in tragedy, it apparently was not easy to live with a child who had been to Buffalo Bill's Wild West.

A Youthful Terror

He has tried to scalp his sister,
    He's lassoed the Thomas cat,
He has shot my English setter
    And tomahawked my hat.
He has frightened his poor mother
    Into forty-seven fits,
He has broken all the ornaments
    Into fifty-seven bits.
Oh! how I rue the day
    That I was made to go
And take my son and heir to see
    That wild and Western show.[11]

Even adults tried to imitate the Wild West. One man gave himself a bloody nose and wrecked his bicycle while trying to grab his hat off the ground in the manner of Cody's Rough Riders. His bicycle crashed into a carriage, the horses ran away, and as in the real Wild West, "a generally exciting time was enjoyed by the spectators."[12]

By 1894 the general structure and particular details of the Wild West were so widely known that 1,300 people could watch and enjoy a burlesque of the show put on in Chicago by Company F, Second Regiment, in a building at the corner of State and Sixteenth Streets. This burlesque featured a band that played "the most martial and soul-stirring music whenever somebody was kicked by a horse or thrown suddenly upon the tanbark," Buffalo Bill hunting bison (represented by kicking burros), and a grand final spectacle.

Chief Big Smoke's tribe of Apaches then attacked the settler's cabin. Company F defeated them, but the Indians forgot to leave the field, and would only disperse when McKenna turned a hose upon them.

The cabin caught fire in the melee and a lively blaze added realism to the scene until extinguished by the same hose just used against the Indians.[13]

This type of imitation was extended to include fads in dress and even in snack foods when the show began touring Europe. In Paris everything, from buckskin suits to Western sunbonnets, was bought and worn after Cody's first summer there. The Stetson hat, first made popular by Cody, became the fashionable headgear for women, and children took whatever was at hand to imitate the dress of the cowboys and Indians. That same year popcorn was introduced by the Wild West, and five tons of it was sold on the grounds.

Even more remarkable than these brief fads was the response of the German people to the Wild West. The German imagination had already been fueled by the dime novels of Karl May, and Cody's show caused an incredible sensation. The German army sent soldiers to take notes on how the show was moved, set up, and torn down again (some of these methods were used in World War I),[14] and hundreds of Western clubs were established to study the West. These clubs are still in operation today, and much time and money are spent each year in preparation for a three-day campout and council competition where the Germans "relive the American frontier days in full dress with almost complete historical veracity."[15] Each of these clubs has been collecting Western artifacts since the 1890s, and the members make a great effort to learn Indian ceremonial dances and songs and the cowboy skills of roping and riding.[16]

Buffalo Bill's Wild West bridged a gap between the original dime novel Westerns of the 1870s and the movie Westerns that began to appear in the 1920s. It coincided with the final settlement of the Western frontier and provided a nostalgic look at the adventure of opening and taming the West. It was the antecedent of comic books, radio shows, television programs, and even other Wild West shows. The show introduced the cowboy, the cowgirl, and most importantly Buffalo Bill Cody into the myth of the American West, and it established the Plains Indian as the symbol for all American Indians in Western iconography.

Seen by millions of people in more than a dozen countries in the 30 years of its existence, the show was a marvel of organization and imagination. Hundreds of performers, staff, and animals were fed, sheltered, and transported each season, and the entire company shared in the difficult task of constructing their performing space, entertaining their audience, and moving their show to a new stand, day after day, year after year. The program of events was a delicate balance of tried events and new acts added to give the show new life, never quite the same from year to year and yet somehow familiar and predictable. With the showmanship and personality of Cody, the careful attention to business details by his managers, and the untiring efforts of the publicity department, the show made millions of dollars and became one of the biggest entertainment enterprises in America.

The major impact of the Wild West was twofold. First, it supported a myth of the American West that gave expression to some of the cultural ideals of turn-of-the-century Americans and so provided an entertaining show. Second, it introduced Americans and Europeans to a new vision of the West, with new character-types, new stories, and new versions of stories already told in other forms. It blended this new vision with the picture of the West already formed by dime novels, melodramas, letters, lectures, and brochures, and encouraged further interest in all things Western. Much information about the Wild West has been lost or forgotten, but the images it created, the characters it introduced, and the interest it sparked have become an important part of the European image of Americans and of America's image of itself.

NOTES

BBHC   Buffalo Bill Historical Center
CS   Cody Scrapbooks
CWM   Circus World Museum
DPL   Denver Public Library
MS   Manuscript
SS   Salsbury Scrapbooks

CHAPTER ONE

1. *London Evening News and Post*, 14 May 1892, CS, BBHC, Cody, Wyo.

2. Don Russell, *The Lives and Legends of Buffalo Bill* (Norman, Okla.: Univ. of Oklahoma Press, 1960), p. 288.

3. Nebraska Ned, *Buffalo Bill and His Daring Adventures in the Romantic Wild West* (Baltimore, Md.: L. and M. Ottenheimer, 1913), pp. 174–75.

4. Russell, *Lives and Legends*, p. 290.

5. John H. Sullivan, *The Life and Adventures of a Cowboy, Broncho John* (Philadelphia: Morrell Bros., 1888).

6. 1883 Program, "W. F. Cody and W. F. Carver's Rocky Mountain and Prairie Exhibition," (n.p.; 1883), DPL, Denver, Colo.

7. Russell, *Lives and Legends*, p. 293.

8. Raymond Thorpe, *Spirit Gun of the West: The Story of Doc W. F. Carver* (Glendale, Calif.: A. H. Clark, 1957), p. 140.

9. Nate Salsbury, "Notes," DPL, MS, in the Salsbury Collection, Denver, Colo.

10. Russell, *Lives and Legends*, p. 309.

11. *Cincinnati Enquirer*, 9 December 1884.

12. Russell, *Lives and Legends* p. 310.

13. 1884 Program, "Buffalo Bill's Wild West," (n.p., 1884), DPL, Denver, Colo.

14. William F. Cody, Letter to John Wallace Crawford, 21 July 1886, William F. Cody Papers, DPL, Denver, Colo.

15. Percy Mackaye, *Epoch: The Life of Steele Mackaye, Genius of the Theatre, In Relation to His Times and Contemporaries* (New York: Boni and Liveright, 1927), p. 76.

16. Ibid., p. 84.

17. *New York Herald*, 30 March 1887, CS, BBHC, Cody, Wyo.

18. Russell, *Lives and Legends* p. 327.

19. Gladys Erskine, *Broncho Charlie: A Saga of the Saddle* (New York: Thomas Y. Crowell, 1934), p. 258.

20. *New York Herald*, n.d., CS, BBHC, Cody, Wyo.

21. *New York Herald*, 19 November 1890, CS, BBHC, Cody, Wyo.

22. Russell, *Lives and Legends*, p. 371.

23. Ibid., p. 375.

24. Ibid., p. 379.

25. Courtney Riley Cooper, "The Story of W. F. Cody, Part III," *Elks Magazine*, July 1927, p. 57.

26. Russell, *Lives and Legends*, p. 443.

27. Cooper, "Story of W. F. Cody," p. 58.

28. 1909 Program, "Buffalo Bill's Wild West and Congress of Rough Riders of the World" (Cincinnati: Strobridge Lithography, 1909), Fitzhaugh Collection, Coe Library, Laramie, Wyo.

29. Cooper, "Story of W. F. Cody," p. 58.

30. Signed 1913 Contract between Cody and Sells-Floto Circus, BBHC, Cody, Wyo.

31. Russell, *Lives and Legends*, p. 456.

32. Court Documents, BBHC, Cody, Wyo.

33. Russell, *Lives and Legends*, p. 464

CHAPTER TWO

1. Harry Webb, Remembrances of the Buffalo Bill Wild West Show, recorded by Harry Webb, September 1982, private collection, two 90–minute cassettes.

2. *Daily British Whig*, Kingston, Ont., 20 August 1885, CS, BBHC, Cody, Wyo.

3. 1896 Route Book, "Buffalo Bill's Wild West and Congress of Rough Riders of the World," (Buffalo, N.Y.: Courier, 1906), pp. 34–35, BBHC, Cody, Wyo.

4. *Fortune*, 21 April 1887, CS, BBHC, Cody, Wyo.

5. Luther Standing Bear, *My People the Sioux* (New York: Houghton Mifflin, 1928), p. 260.

6. *London Tid-Bits*, 28 May 1892, and unidentified newspaper clippings, in CS, BBHC, Cody, Wyo.

7. "Newspaper Men in Battle," unidentified Boston paper, 15 June 1899, in CS, BBHC, Cody, Wyo.

8. 1896 Route Book, p. 274.

9. Harry Webb, "Buffalo Bill and Me," *Westerner*, August 1971, p. 38.

10. Annie Swartwout, *Missie* (Bianchester, Ohio: Brown Publishing, 1947), p. 232.

11. Reminiscences of Ed Kelly, Guernsey, as told to TPW. Wyoming State Archives, Cheyenne, Wyo., Cody File, B-C649–wf.

12. *The Cody Enterprise*, 4 July 1968, p. 13.

13. Harry Webb, "My Year with Buffalo Bill's Wild West Show," Part 1, *Real West* 13, no. 78 (January 1970), 54.

14. "Electricity at the Wild West Show," *The Electric World* 13, no. 11 (September 1894), 253–54, CS, BBHC, Cody, Wyo.

15. Ibid.

16. *Brooklyn Standard Union*, 7 July 1894, CS, BBHC, Cody, Wyo.

17. Ibid.

18. *New York Recorder*, 11 June 1894, SS, DPL, Denver, Colo.

19. A bucking strap is a leather strap fastened around the horse's belly that irritates the horse into bucking for a short period of time.

20. *London Tid-Bits*, 28 May 1892. CS, BBHS, Cody, Wyo.

21. *The Long Branch Press*, 7 June 1899, SS, DPL, Denver, Colo.

22. *Cardiff Mail*, 18 June 1903, CS, BBHC, Cody, Wyo.

23. Jack Rennert, *100 Posters of Buffalo Bill's Wild West* (New York: Darien House, 1976), p. 5.

24. Ibid.

25. Charles Fox and Tom Parkinson, *The Circus in America* (Waukesha, Wisc.: Country Beautiful, 1969), p. 158; and letter received by author from Harry Webb, 21 March 1983.

26. Ibid.

27. Fox and Parkinson, *The Circus*, p. 160.

CHAPTER THREE

1. 1898 Program, "Buffalo Bill's Wild West and Congress of Rough Riders of the World," (New York: Fless and Ridge Printing, 1898), DPL, Denver, Colo.

2. Harry Webb, "Buffalo Bill and Me," *Westerner*, July/August 1971, p. 38.

3. *New York Advertiser*, 20 May 1894, CS, BBHC, Cody, Wyo.

4. *Daily Spectator and Tribune* [Hamilton, Ont.], 27 August 1885, CS, BBHC, Cody, Wyo.

5. *Brooklyn Times*, 7 July 1894, SS, DPL, Denver, Colo.

6. Unidentified clipping, Johnny Baker scrapbook, DPL, Denver, Colo.

7. *Baltimore Star*, 20 April 1911, CS, BBHC, Cody, Wyo.

8. Captain Bogardus was the inventor of the spring trap which throws glass balls or clay pigeons into the air to simulate the actual flight of birds.

9. Don Russell, *The Lives and Legends of Buffalo Bill* (Norman, Okla.: Univ. of Oklahoma Press, 1960), p. 318.

10. Ibid.

11. Courtney Riley Cooper, *Annie Oakley, Woman at Arms* (New York: Duffield and Co., 1927), p. 120.

12. Captain Frank Winch, "Was Buffalo Bill a Fake Shot?," *Field and Stream*, October 1920, p. 574.

13. Cooper, *Annie Oakley*, p. 133.

14. Russell, *Lives and Legends*, p. 319.

15. *Free Press and Times* [Burlington, Vt.], 6 August 1885, CS, BBHC, Cody, Wyo.

16. *Baltimore Star*, 20 April 1911, CS, BBHC, Cody, Wyo.

17. Webb, "Buffalo Bill and Me," p. 38.

18. 1913 Program, "Buffalo Bill's Wild West and Pawnee Bill's Far East Combined," (Buffalo, N.Y.: Courier, 1913), CWM, Baraboo, Wisc.

19. 1903 Program, "Buffalo Bill's Wild West and Congress of Rough Riders of the World," (Buffalo, N.Y.: Courier 1903), CWM, Baraboo, Wisc.

20. Unidentified newspaper article, 28 April 1910, CS, BBHC, Cody, Wyo.

21. *Baltimore Star*, 20 August 1911, CS, BBHC, Cody, Wyo.

22. Clippings, CS, SS, and Baker Scrapbooks, DPL, Denver, Colo.

23. Charles Griffin, *Four Years in Europe with Buffalo Bill* (Albia, Iowa: Stage Publishing, 1908), p. 93.

24. Russell, *Lives and Legends*, p. 381.

25. Jack Rennert, *100 Posters of Buffalo Bill's Wild West* (New York: Darien House, 1976), p. 14.

26. *Sportsman*, 27 December 1903, CS, BBHC, Cody, Wyo.

27. *Plebian*, 11 June 1892, SS, DPL, Denver, Colo.

28. Clifford Westermeier, *Trailing the Cowboy* (Caldwell, Idaho: Caxton Printers, 1955), p. 86.

29. 1896 Route Book, "Buffalo Bill's Wild West and Congress of Rough Riders of the World," (Buffalo, N.Y.: Courier, 1896).

30. *The Standard,* 10 May 1887, CS, BBHC, Cody, Wyo.

31. Joyce Roach, *The Cowgirls* (Houston, Tex.: Cordoval, 1977), p. 118.

32. Russell, *Lives and Legends,* p. 226.

33. *Mail Express,* 16 May 1894, SS, DPL, Denver, Colo.

34. *The Antex Ocean* [Chicago], 7 September 1897, SS, DPL, Denver, Colo.

35. *New York Journal,* 31 May 1898, CS, BBHC, Cody, Wyo.

36. *Baltimore Star,* 20 August 1911, CS, BBHC, Cody, Wyo.

37. Russell, *Lives and Legends,* p. 458.

38. *The Evening Sun* [New York], 7 April 1901, SS, DPL, Denver, Colo.

39. Russell, *Lives and Legends,* p. 419.

40. 1901 Program, "Buffalo Bill's Wild West and Congress of Rough Riders of the World," (Buffalo, N.Y.: Courier, 1901), DPL, Denver, Colo.

41. Russell, *Lives and Legends,* p. 419.

42. 1909 Courier, "Buffalo Bill's Wild West and Congress of Rough Riders of the World," (n.p; 1909), DPL, Denver, Colo.

43. 1908 Program, "Buffalo Bill's Wild West and Congress of Rough Riders of the World," (Buffalo, N.Y.: Courier, 1908), CWM, Baraboo, Wisc.

44. *St. James Gazette,* 28 July 1892, and Newcastle *Daily Journal,* both in CS, BBHC, Cody, Wyo.

45. 1907 Indian Head Courier, "Buffalo Bill's Wild West and Congress of Rough Riders of the World," (n.p.; 1907), DPL, Denver, Colo.

46. Ibid.

47. Harry Webb, "My Year with Buffalo Bill's Wild West Show," Part 1, *Real West* 13, no. 78 (Janaury 1970): 55.

48. Shannon Garst, *Buffalo Bill* (New York: J. Messner, 1948), pp. 165–66.

49. *Cincinnati Enquirer,* 12 September 1894, SS, DPL, Denver, Colo.

50. *Era,* 30 July 1892, n.p., SS, DPL, Denver, Colo.

51. Griffin, *Four Years in Europe,* p. 28.

CHAPTER FOUR

1. Charles Griffin, *Four Years in Europe with Buffalo Bill* (Albia, Iowa: Stage Publishing, 1908), p. 56.

2. Con Groner was sheriff of North Platte, Nebraska. He broke up Doc Middleton's gang and participated in a number of other notable arrests. David Payne was the organizer of the Oklahoma "Boomers" who wished the Oklahoma Indian Territory opened to homesteaders.

3. All information about contracts is based on several blank and completed contracts contained in the Wild West Show collection in the Western History Collection of the Denver Public Library and on a signed contract in the collection at Scout's Rest Ranch, North Platte, Nebraska.

4. *Pall Mall Bud*, 9 June 1892, SS, DPL, Denver, Colo.

5. Earl May, *The Circus from Rome to Ringling* (New York: Dover Publications, 1963), p. x.

6. *London Star*, 31 May 1892, CS, BBHC, Cody, Wyo.

7. *Era*, 11 June 1892, SS, DPL, Denver, Colo.

8. *Saturday Review*, 2 July 1892, SS, DPL, Denver, Colo.

9. *Army and Navy Gazette*, 11 June 1892, CS, BBHC, Cody, Wyo.

10. *New York Daily News*, 2 June 1892, SS, DPL, Denver, Colo.

11. *New York Herald*, 10 May 1894, CS, BBHC, Cody, Wyo.

12. 1907 Indian Head Courier, "Buffalo Bill's Wild West and Congress of Rough Riders of the World," (n.p.; 1907), DPL, Denver, Colo.

13. John Nelson, *Fifty Years on the Trail: a True Story of Western Life* (Norman, Okla.: Univ. of Oklahoma Press, 1963), p. viii.

14. *Cincinnati Enquirer*, 12 September 1894, SS, DPL, Denver, Colo.

15. Les Kennon, "He Didn't Spank Me," *True West* 9, no. 3 (Janaury-February 1962): 52.

16. *Morning*, 18 August 1892, SS, DPL, Denver, Colo.

17. *New York Morning Journal*, 28 April 1889, CS, BBHC, Cody, Wyo.

18. 1896, 1899, 1902, and 1911 Route Books.

19. Daniel Dorchester, "62nd Annual Report of the Commissioner of Indian Affairs," in U.S. Congress, *House Executive Documents*, No. 1, Pt. 5, 53rd Congress 2nd Sess., p. 395.

20. *New York Herald*, 30 November 1890, CS, BBHC, Cody, Wyo.

21. Raymond Thorpe, *Spirit Gun of the West: The Story of Doc W. F. Carver.* (Glendale, Calif.: A. H. Clark, 1957), p. 180.

22. John G. Neihardt, *Black Elk Speaks* (New York: Pocket Books, 1972), pp. 182–83.

23. Don Russell, *The Wild West: A History of the Wild West Shows* (Fort Worth, Tex.: Amon Carter Museum of Western Art, 1970), p. 67.

24. U.S. Bureau of Statistics, *Statistical Abstract of the United States 1908* (Washington, D.C.: Government Printing Office, 1909), p. 235.

25. Don Russell, *The Lives and Legends of Buffalo Bill* (Norman, Okla: Univ. of Oklahoma Press, 1960), p. 316.

26. Neihardt, *Black Elk Speaks*, pp. 185–86.

27. Rupert Croft-Cooke and W. S. Meadmore, *Buffalo Bill: The Legend, the Man of Action, the Showman* (London: Sidgwick and Jackson, 1952), p. 85.

28. Russell, *Lives and Legends*, p. 420.

29. Ibid., p. 458. There are no complete copies of the film made of

Wounded Knee still in existence. Several of the other films still exist in private collections around the country.

30. Jim Doherty, "The Last of the Great Scouts is Back Again," *Smithsonian*, January 1983, p. 62.

31. Jack Rennert, *100 Posters of Buffalo Bill's Wild West* (New York: Darien House, 1976), p. 4.

32. William Frederick Cody, Letter to Bell, 18 November 1908, Cody Letters, Western History Collection, DPL, Denver, Colo.

33. Nebraska Ned, *Buffalo Bill and His Daring Adventures in the Romantic Wild West* (Baltimore, Md.: L. and M. Ottenheimer, 1913), pp. 180–81.

34. Don Holm, "Were There Two Buffalo Bills?," *Frontier Times* 39, no. 5 (August-September 1965): 35–36.

35. "Trooper's Dad Pal of Buffalo Bill," *The Sunday Telegram*, n.d., Cody Letter ff6, DPL, Denver, Colo.

36. Rennert, *100 Posters*, p. 9.

CHAPTER FIVE

1. *Stevens Point Daily Journal*, 5 September 1896, SS, DPL, Denver, Colo.

2. The checks at the Buffalo Bill Historical Center are canceled personal checks of Cody's and cover the entire thirty years of the show. Unfortunately, no entire year is represented, and there are only a few checks for several years during the period. A personal check for $10,000 from Cody to Lillie dated February 1, 1913, is included in this collection. It is almost certainly the money Cody borrowed from Harry Tammen to pay wintering costs for the show, which finally put an end to Buffalo Bill's Wild West.

The checks at the University of Oklahoma are all printed on Wild West stationery and are all written by or for Gordon W. Lillie and Thomas Smith.

3. Nellie Snyder Yost, *Buffalo Bill: His Family, Friends, Fame, Failures, and Fortunes* (Chicago: Sage Books, 1979), p. 156.

4. 1899 Route Book, "Buffalo Bill's Wild West and Congress of Rough Riders of the World," (Buffalo, N.Y.: Mathews-Northrup, 1899), BBHC, Cody, Wyo.

5. Canceled checks, Johnny Baker materials, BBHC, Cody, Wyo.

6. Canceled checks, Gordon Lillie Collection, Univ. of Oklahoma, Norman, Okla., and BBHC, Cody, Wyo.

7. 1886 Program, "Buffalo Bill's Wild West," (Hartford, Conn.: Calhoun Printing, 1886), DPL, Denver, Colo.

8. *London Tid-Bits*, 28 May 1892, CS, BBHC, Cody, Wyo.

9. Weekly Statement, "Buffalo Bill's Wild West and Pawnee Bill's Far East Combined," Gordon Lillie Collection, Univ. of Oklahoma, Norman, Okla.

10. *The Sunday Call* [Easton, Pa.], 12 August 1894, n.p., SS, DPL, Denver, Colo.

11. 1907 Program, "Buffalo Bill's Wild West and Congress of Rough Riders of the World," (Cincinnati: Strobridge Lithography, 1907), Fitzhaugh Collection, Coe Library, Laramie, Wyo.

12. 1886 Program.

13. 1911 Route Book, "Buffalo Bill's Wild West Pawnee Bill's Far East Combined," (n.p.; 1911), BBHC, Cody, Wyo.

14. Herbert Cody Blake, *Blake's Western Stories* (Brooklyn, N.Y.: H. C. Blake, 1929), p. 30.

15. Don Russell, *The Lives and Legends of Buffalo Bill* (Norman, Okla.: Univ. of Oklahoma Press, 1960), p. 302.

16. *Pittsburgh Leader*, 8 July 1894, SS, DPL, Denver, Colo.

CHAPTER SIX

1. Paul Bouissac, *Circus and Culture. A Semiotic Approach* (Bloomington, Ind.: Indiana Univ. Press, 1976), pp. 14–15. I am indebted to Bouissac for the models of analyzing circus performance put forth in his book.

2. Ibid., pp. 25–26. Although this model was prepared for analyzing circus performances, it applies as it stands to the Wild West.

3. Keir Elam, *Semiotics of Theatre and Drama* (London: Methuen, 1980), p. 26.

4. Bouissac, *Circus and Culture*, pp. 90–91.

5. Ibid., p. 71. See Chapter 5, "On Jugglers and Magicians," for further descriptions of jugglers and juggling.

6. Robert Toll, *On With the Show* (New York: Oxford Univ. Press, 1976), p. 52.

7. Bouissac, *Circus and Culture*, p. 130.

8. See ibid., p. 13, for a brief discussion of how circus acts are chosen and ordered.

CHAPTER SEVEN

1. Marie, Queen of Rumania, "Wyoming. Oh! West of West!" Cody File, Wyoming State Archives, Cheyenne, Wyo. Written by hand on royal stationery. The poem is not dated but must be prior to 1907 when Cody returned to America after his last tour of Europe, and may be as

early as 1887 when many of the European royalty viewed the Wild West as a part of Queen Victoria's Jubilee.

2. Elizabeth Lawrence, *Rodeo: An Anthropological Look at the Wild and the Tame* (Knoxville, Tenn.: Univ. of Tennessee Press, 1982), p. 48.

3. William Judson, "The Movies," in *Buffalo Bill and the Wild West* (Brooklyn, N.Y.: The Brooklyn Museum, 1981), p. 26.

4. Warren French, "The Cowboy in the Dime Novel," *Studies in English* 30 (1951): 229–30.

5. Joyce Roach, *The Cowgirls* (Houston, Tex.: Cordoval, 1977), p. 141.

6. Don Russell, *The Lives and Legends of Buffalo Bill* (Norman, Okla.: Univ. of Oklahoma Press, 1960), p. 384.

7. Jack Rennert, *100 Posters of Buffalo Bill's Wild West* (New York: Darien House, 1976), p. 3.

8. *New York Advertiser*, 27 June 1894, CS, BBHC, Cody, Wyo.

9. Chauncey Yellow Robe, "The Menace of the Wild West Show," *Quarterly Journal of the Society of American Indians* 2 (July-September, 1914): 225.

10. *Brooklyn Times*, 10 September 1894, CS, BBHC, Cody, Wyo.

11. *New York World*, 24 June 1894, CS, BBHC, Cody, Wyo.

12. *Chicago Bearins*, 1 June 1894, SS, DPL, Denver, Colo.

13. *Chicago Tribune*, 17 June 1894, SS, DPL, Denver, Colo.

14. Paul O'Neil, *The End and the Myth*, vol. 26 of *The Old West* (Alexandria, Va.: Time-Life Books, 1979), p. 74.

15. "Sie Ritten Da'Lang Podner," *Time*, 18 June 1979, p. 17.

16. O'Neil, *The End and the Myth*, p. 78.

BIBLIOGRAPHICAL ESSAY

Primary source material for research on this topic is so scattered and so varied that I have chosen not to list each individual item, but rather to include a short listing of collections and types of materials that researchers might find useful.

The three major public collections of Wild West materials are held by the Denver Public Library in Denver, Colorado; the Circus World Museum in Baraboo, Wisconsin; and the Buffalo Bill Historical Center in Cody, Wyoming. Additional material on the 101 Wild West and Pawnee Bill's Wild West can be found in the University of Oklahoma archives in Norman, Oklahoma. There are many private collections mostly held as part of larger circus collections that contain varying amounts of primary material as well.

This primary source material falls into five main categories:

1. Material printed by the show, such as programs, couriers, route books, and various souvenir booklets
2. Contemporary newspaper accounts found in the many volumes of scrapbooks kept by Cody and other members of the Wild West companies (most are in the collections of the Buffalo Bill Historical Center)
3. Personal remembrances of people who traveled with or saw the show such as oral history tapes, letters, or manuscripts
4. Ledger books, financial statements, and checks
5. Photographs and film footage of the show

Hundreds of volumes have been written about William F. Cody and all of them contain some measure of information on the Wild West. Several excellent and exhaustive bibliographies of this material already exist and it seems needless to include all my references here. Instead I have chosen to include only a few listings that will prove most useful to an interested reader.

The most useful references for any scholar studying the Wild West are Mr. Don Russell's two books *The Lives and Legends of Buffalo Bill* (Norman, Okla.: Univ. of Oklahoma Press, 1960) and *The Wild West: A*

History of Wild West Shows (Fort Worth, Tex.: Amon Carter Museum of Western Art, 1970). The former is by far the best biography of Cody and contains an extensive bibliography, while the latter gives a good general overview of the phenomenon of the Wild West and includes dozens of fine photographs.

I found Jack Rennert's *100 Posters of Buffalo Bill's Wild West* (New York: Darien House, 1976) extremely helpful, both because the text includes some descriptions of Wild West events and because the beautifully reproduced posters help identify prevalent Wild West images.

For more specific information about Indians and their experiences in the show I direct the reader to the following books. To gain a good general background on the display of Indians the best source is Carolyn Foreman's *Indians Abroad* (Norman, Okla.: Univ. of Oklahoma Press, 1943). If the reader is more interested in the feelings of the Indians being exhibited I highly recommend John Neihardt's *Black Elk Speaks* (New York: Pocket Books, 1972), and *My People the Sioux* (New York: Houghton Miflin, 1928) by Luther Standing Bear.

Raymond Thorpe's book *Spirit Gun of the West: The Story of Doc W.F. Carver* (Glendale, Calif.: A.H. Clark, 1957), which is really a biography of Doc Carver, provides an interesting view of Cody and the early years of the Wild West because it presents Buffalo Bill in an almost entirely negative light.

For those particularly interested in the logistics of setting up, tearing down, and moving the show the best easy reference is *The Circus in America* (Wankesha, Wisc.: Country Beautiful, 1969) by Chappie Fox and Tom Parkinson.

In order to truly understand Cody's position as both a mythic hero and an image maker, the scholar should understand the other forces that were helping to create the myth of the American West. Ray Billington's study *Land of Savagery, Land of Promise* (New York: Norton, 1981) does an excellent job of exploring the effect of the many movements involved in this process.

In addition to the many books dealing with William F. Cody and his life, there are hundreds of magazine articles to be considered.

The most reliable articles appear in state historical journals such as *Annals of Wyoming, Nebraska History*, or *Wisconsin Magazine of History*. The publications of *The Westerners* are also good sources of information. Such magazines as *National Geographic, The Smithsonian, Journal of Popular Culture, Bandwagon*, and *American West* publish well-researched, up-to-date information periodically.

Less scholarly, but perhaps more interesting, material often appears in such magazines as *True West, Frontier Times*, and *Old West*. These are usually accounts by people who either rode with a Wild West or were somehow involved in the operation of the show.

This list is by no means exhaustive, as such a list would have burdened the reader with a huge number of references that few people would be interested in pursuing. I would be pleased to identify the sources for my statements and quotations to anyone who inquires.

INDEX

veterans, 64
villains, 6, 7
"The Virginia Reel on Horseback," 67, 119, 130

Waldron, Nelse, 18
war paint, use of, 78
Western girls. *See* cowgirls
The Western Girl, 90
Westmore, Helen Cody (Cody's
  sister), 96
Whirling dervish, 79
Whitaker, Ma and Pa, 84
White Horse, 25
"Wild Texas Steer," 62
Wild West, 15, 18, 37, 129; acts
  relating to circus acts, 112; attendance to, 95; auctioned off,
  92; blacks performing in, 62;
  care of livestock in, 48; categories of acts, 54; costs, 18;
  cost of food/commodities, 47;
  as dramatic spectacles, 68;
  early venues of, 37; earnings
  of, 97; equipment of, 43; expenses of, 96; financing of, 29,
  30; first opening of, 14; first
  touring of, 13; first trip to
  England of, 21; food for, 41,
  42, 47, 90; impact of, 134; in
  transition, 17; incorporation,
  21; James Bailey joins management of, 27; large venues, 38;
management of, 98; military
  acts in, 63; organization of,
  97–101; originators' claims to,
  11; performers' origins, 79;
  other Wild Wests, 8; put up
  for auction, 2; races in, 57; relation to circus, 8, 62, 117; relation to rodeo, 8, 13; return
  to Europe (1902), 28; riding
  events in, 65; Salsbury's influence on, 28; sharpshooting
  acts in, 58; show is attached,
  33; specialty acts in, 61, 63;
  stand in Paris of, 24; success
  wanes, 27, 28; successes of, 3,
  18, 22, 26; tents and canvas
  needed for, 42; tour of Europe by, 26
Winch, Frank, 60
Winert, Paul (Wounded Knee
  survivor), 83
Women, 68, 79, 83, 84. *See also*
  cowgirls
Women bronc riders, 68
World War I, 2
World's Fair of 1893 (Chicago),
  3, 26–27
World's Industrial and Cotton
  Exposition, 16

Yankee Film Company, 93
Yellow Hair, 69, 128
Yellowstone Park, 2, 91, 92

About the Author

SARAH J. BLACKSTONE is Assistant Professor and Director of Theatre at the University of Central Arkansas, Conway. She has written for *Bandwagon: Journal of the Circus Historical Society.*